"Without a strategy, a few of your videos might perform. But with a smart strategy, many will connect with the right people and be watched to the end. And when that happens, your business grows.

Follow the wisdom in Ben's book and build your own successful video strategy."

—*Michael Stelzner, Founder of Social Media Examiner and Social Media Marketing World*

"*Engage* is a must-read for anyone looking to master video marketing. With 14 years of expertise under his belt, Ben provides a clear, actionable guide to crafting effective video strategies. From audience targeting to practical marketing insights, real-world case studies and essential tools—it's all covered.

Whether you're new to video marketing or a seasoned pro, this book will help you create compelling content that converts!"

—*Chris Ducker, Bestselling author of 'Rise of the Youpreneur'*

"The One Page Video Strategy Canvas is magnificent. Having that one tool in my video strategy toolkit makes it easy to win."

—*James Schramko, JamesSchramko.com, Author of 'Work Less, Make More'*

"*Engage* is an actionable blueprint to guide effective video production that returns tangible results. Ben Amos is a leading expert in the field of video marketing and *Engage* is a book that I feel confident using in my social media content creation course at University of the Sunshine Coast and will also refer my clients to."

—*Dr Karen Sutherland, University of the Sunshine Coast and Dharana Digital*

"Written with humour and filled with actionable insights, Ben Amos's new book *Engage* had me hooked—and laughing—from the first page. This book is for anyone who has created a video because 'everyone is doing video'. And yes, despite being a strategist for over twenty years, this includes me. Oh, the irony.

Engage is a practical guide that follows a simple framework so you too can implement a strategic approach to your video marketing. It's a must-read for business owners who want to create video content that attracts, engages and converts."

—*Mel Kettle, Leadership Communication Strategist, Speaker, Author, Facilitator*

"Ben's seven-step video strategy framework is both practical and powerful. Since implementing it, I've delivered measurable results for my clients and strengthened my role as a true strategic partner. *Engage* is a must-read for anyone wanting to elevate their video marketing approach."

—*Bill Baroana, Founder, Flex Media - Ohio, USA*

"Having seen Ben speak on several occasions I knew his book would be amazing.

Not only does it offer practical ideas that normal humans can actually implement, its use of case studies and examples makes it all feel totally doable.

I'm not a strategy person, but this book could persuade me! Especially the whole one-page approach. Ben's clear and likeable writing style sucks you in, and I found myself making copious notes.

A great read for those wanting to make video a working part of their overall marketing."

—*Kate Toon, Author of 'Six Figures While You Sleep'*

"It's so easy to get caught up in just producing video content or focusing on tech. But without a strategy, we're almost guaranteed to miss the mark. Engage fills this gap. Ben helps us create the right videos for the right audience. Packed with actionable insights, it's clear, approachable, and refreshingly fun—a must-read for anyone serious about video success."

—*Ian Anderson Gray, Host of the Smart AI Podcast, Confident Live Marketing Podcast and Smart ADHD Podcast*

"Every business needs videos that convert! This book lays out an action plan for creating a range of videos to get you an incredible return on your investment when you focus on strategy, not tactics, and a whole lot more. Highly recommended!"

—*Greg Merrilees, Owner, Studio1Design.com*

engage

THE DEFINITIVE GUIDE TO VIDEO STRATEGY FOR BUSINESS

BEN AMOS

Published by Innovate Media

innovatemedia.com.au

ISBN-13: 978-1-7637919-0-9

Cover design by Kelly Exeter and Ben Amos

Interior design by Kelly Exeter

This book is ultimately dedicated to you—the reader, the future Video Strategist, the action-taker.

But underneath everything, as an author and a businessman, lies a bedrock foundation upon which everything is built. That is my wife, Nicole and two daughters Eloise and Skye. You're my why.

Contents

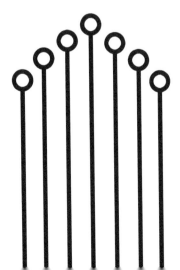

BONUS MATERIAL

For downloadable worksheets and resources,
scan the QR code below.

engage

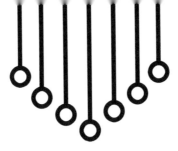

INTRODUCTION

Have you heard of the term BFO? It stands for:

Blinding.

Flash.

Of the Obvious.

For me, a significant BFO happened in 2016. And it changed the course of my business.

I'd started my professional career in education, teaching film and media production to high school students. After a while though, it felt like I was spending more time managing behaviours and dealing with administrative bureaucracy than I was actually teaching.

I needed a change, and (you know how it is …) the idea of being my own boss seemed like the ultimate path to unending riches and glory. So I decided to start my own video production business.

All I needed to start a video business was a high-definition video camera, a few accessories … and, of course, a computer capable of editing videos. I tallied up the capital needed to get started, and it came to $15,000.

Damn.

My teacher's salary wasn't going to help me there.

I had just finished paying off the credit card debt that had accumulated after my earlier years of travelling and working in the UK and I didn't want to go down that road again.

So I went to my local business banker, armed with an impressively bound copy of my exciting business plan (colour printed and all), and requested a start-up loan.

They refused my application almost immediately. (Although they did offer me the chance to take out a personal loan at a stupidly high interest rate. Banks are so generous.)

So I had to resort to Plan B. El Banco Familia.

(That would be the Bank of Mum and Dad. Thanks, Mum and Dad.)

Armed with my new camera gear and Mac Pro tower, I went in search of someone to pay me to make them a video.

That kicked off a six-year journey of weddings, events, 16mm film to digital conversions, photo slideshows, training DVDs and even the occasional logo design. I did anything anyone would pay me to do that was loosely related to video.

Then in 2016, the BFO happened.

INTRODUCTION

I remember the client well. A local furniture removalist paid me to produce a few brand videos for them. I planned out a great shoot, conducted compelling interviews with the business owner and some of their clients, shot some beautiful footage, and edited fantastic brand videos for them.

I loved the videos. The client loved the videos. I got paid, and I moved on to find the next client willing to let me make a video for them.

No problems, right?

Not quite.

Six months after completing the job, I checked back to see what the client had done with their videos. I went to their website and saw a small YouTube video sitting embedded in the top right corner of the homepage.

'Okay,' I thought. 'It's a bit small up there, but at least they've got it online.'

Then I clicked through to the YouTube watch page, and saw the view count.

34 views.

Ergh.

I felt like I'd been punched in the gut. 34 views meant my client was getting almost zero return on the investment they'd made in my services. Worse, it was likely that the majority of those views were from the client themselves ... and their Mum.

This was the point where I realised I was failing my clients.

Something needed to change.

It wasn't the video itself that failed. It was the lack of strategy behind it.

No one, including my client, had discussed how the video was going to get the results they wanted, what they were going to do with the video when they had it, or even if it was the right video to produce in the first place!

This was when I realised it wasn't a video that my clients wanted.

They wanted the RESULTS that the right video, used the right way online would get for their business.

This BFO made me realise I needed to be more for my clients than just another video producer. I needed to guide and help them develop the right plan for their business to grow using video.

This kicked off my journey to becoming a confident Video Strategist. (This term didn't really exist in 2016, but I'm proud to have helped make it mainstream over the last few years.)

I dove in deep from that point forward. Feverishly consuming as much information as I could about marketing strategy, advertising principles, digital platform best practice, human behaviour, sales psychology and more.

I read books and articles, listened to podcasts, attended conferences, completed courses and learnt from some of the best marketers in the world. I then brought those ideas and principles to the work my business was doing for our clients.

INTRODUCTION

Most importantly, I developed what I was learning and practising into a framework so I could more easily share these ideas with my clients and with my team. This was the point when other video producers in my network began asking questions about what I was doing with video strategy so they could implement the same things for their clients.

This framework, The Engage Framework, is built on seven core elements and acts as a comprehensive but easy to navigate roadmap for effective video strategy. The Engage Framework has been refined, updated and expanded over the subsequent years as more and more businesses have adopted the approach, and as other Video Strategists across the world have introduced the Engage methodology to their own clients.

What you'll discover as you continue through this book is a complete breakdown of what constitutes an effective video strategy for a business.

Part 1 will help you understand the state of video for business right now, and gain a deeper appreciation for why video strategy is more important today than ever before. I'll share with you the key distinction between strategy and tactics and why so many businesses (including professional video producers) are approaching video marketing the wrong way. You'll reframe your view of video and adopt a Video Strategist mindset. You'll not only see video as a tool for business growth, you'll also be armed with the language and confidence to help others see the future for video in your organisation through the same lens that you do. You'll be equipped to communicate the true value of the videos you'll be creating in your business, and, most importantly, how the right videos, for the right purpose, used in the right way will set your video strategy up for incredible return on investment (ROI).

In Part 2, we'll unpack the seven core elements the Engage Framework is built on and explore how each of these elements connects and derives context from the others.

Part 3 is where you'll be empowered to put theory into practice via the three Engage tools: The 7-minute Video Marketing Strategy, The Engage One Page Video Strategy Canvas and The Simple 7.

Finally, I will share real-world business case studies from businesses across a range of industries who are dominating in their niche through the use of strategic videos. When you read about these businesses putting the concepts in this book into real-world action and tangible business results, I've no doubt you'll be inspired to do the same for your own business or that of your clients.

Are you ready to grow as a confident Video Strategist?

Let's engage!

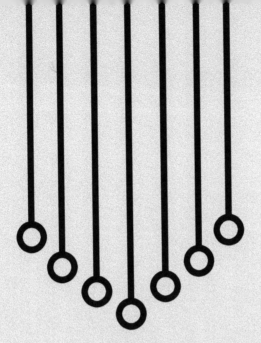

PART 1

Get Ready to Engage

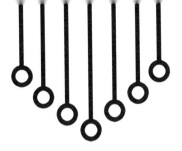

CHAPTER 1

A quick history lesson

It may not feel like it, but video has been a 'thing' online for over 20 years now.

The earliest use of video occurred at a time when the internet was predominantly text-based, sprinkled with occasional pictures. During the late 1990s and early 2000s, while the concept of sharing videos online existed, it was fraught with challenges. Remember, this was the era before broadband became widespread. Many users were still grappling with dial-up connections that beeped and whirred before granting access to the digital world. Consequently, videos were often grainy and pixelated, with lengthy buffer times and limited accessibility.

Various platforms attempted to carve a niche for themselves, with some success. RealPlayer and Windows Media Player became popular tools to play videos, but they were primarily used for downloaded content rather than streaming. Apple's QuickTime also made a notable mark. Websites like

AtomFilms and iFilm catered to short film enthusiasts. But these early platforms were more repositories than communities. The need for a space where users could easily upload, share and discover videos was palpable.

Tune In, Hook Up

In 2005, three former PayPal employees—Chad Hurley, Steve Chen and Jawed Karim—came together with an idea for a video-based dating site, with a cheeky tagline reported to read 'Tune In, Hook Up'. The premise was simple: users would upload short video profiles introducing themselves and describing what they were looking for in a partner. Other users could then watch these profiles and connect if they were interested.

The 'Tune In, Hook Up' iteration of YouTube didn't take off. As tends to be the case with these things, the founders quickly realised that while users were not so keen on the dating angle, they were intrigued by the video-sharing aspect. The trio noticed that people wanted to share videos from a wide range of categories—from home videos and holiday clips to news snippets and music performances. Sensing an opportunity, they pivoted, shedding the dating aspect of the site and transforming their platform into a general video-sharing site.

In April 2005, 'Me at the zoo' by Jawed Karim was the first video uploaded to the new video-sharing site. This 19-second clip, featuring Karim at the San Diego Zoo, may seem mundane by today's standards, but it signalled the birth of something monumental. By November 2005, just a few months after its official launch, YouTube had already secured a $3.5 million investment from Sequoia Capital. The word spread, and users flocked.

It was YouTube's simplicity that set it apart. For the first time, individuals had an easy way to share moments, creativity and insights without the need for specialised software or in-depth technical know-how. This ease of use, combined with the burgeoning growth of broadband connections, allowed YouTube to flourish.

By 2006, big-name corporations began to take note of the site's meteoric rise. Google, recognising the potential, acquired YouTube for a staggering $1.65 billion in stock. This was a move that signalled the undeniable cultural and economic value of online video. And it is no surprise that the world of online video for business began to take hold from there, although at that time only for the true early adopters.

The rise of the Video Strategist

Fast forward a bit from the above and you get to a time in the late 2000s/early 2010s where technology caught up with the demands of video and streaming video on websites and across newly developed social media platforms became more mainstream.

It was around 2007 that I and others started calling ourselves Video Strategists. As brands started investing more in video online, the need for experts who could guide these investments strategically became evident.

What is a Video Strategist? As with many things, it depends who you ask. But if you're asking me, I would say it's someone who typically helps brands, companies or individuals plan, execute and optimise video content for specific goals (whether that's brand awareness, engagement, sales or customer loyalty). This role has become especially crucial with the explosion of video content on platforms like YouTube, LinkedIn, Facebook, Instagram, TikTo, and more. Given the overwhelming amount of video content available and the importance of video in today's digital landscape, having a strategy in place is essential for standing out and achieving desired outcomes.

A Video Strategist might:

- **Assess a brand's target audience and goals:** Before creating content, it's crucial to understand what the brand hopes to achieve and who they're trying to reach.

- **Develop a content plan:** This could involve determining the types of videos to create, their length, style and tone.

- **Determine preferred distribution channels and methods:** With an increasingly complex digital landscape, the options for publishing and distributing video content online need expert guidance and clear direction for maximum success.

- **Optimise for platforms:** Different platforms have different best practices. A video that works on YouTube might not be as effective on TikTok or Instagram. A strategist will understand these nuances.

- **Measure and analyse performance:** Using analytics tools, they can determine which videos are resonating with audiences and which aren't. Based on analytics and audience feedback, they might suggest tweaks to future video content or a shift in strategy.
- **Guide video production style and approach:** With a defined strategy in play, the act of producing the right video content using the right production styles and approaches is critical for success. From big budget productions with highly creative concepts, through to DIY videos on smartphones or user-generated content collated from a community, a Video Strategist is equipped to guide production for optimal results and return on investment.

You are a Video Strategist

Whether you're a founder or director, in the C-suite, marketing, sales, customer success or even a microbusiness owner wearing multiple hats, becoming a confident Video Strategist will give you a skillset that will serve you well as the world of communications and business moves even faster towards a video-first approach.

While you might not be planning to print the title on your business card, or in your email footer, having the mindset of a Video Strategist simply means you believe in the power of video done right—video that is produced, distributed and monetised in the right way, aligned to genuine business goals.

This book will give you the confidence to take your knowledge and experience as a Video Strategist to the next level. I'm stoked for the journey you're about to begin.

Some who read this book will take the ideas, concepts and frameworks and apply them to their own business outcomes. If this is you, then I'm so glad you've got this book in your hands, as the insights you'll gain will be instrumental in your future business success when you embrace the framework outlined in Part 2 and use the tools shared in Part 3.

Others reading this book are seeking to better serve their clients and customers through video strategy. Perhaps you're an agency owner, a video producer, a social media marketer or a content creator. Your goal as you adopt the approaches, frameworks, templates and strategies in these pages is to execute on behalf of your clients, or to guide them to success for their businesses through effective video strategy. If this is you, then you are undoubtedly very similar to the position I was in over eight years before writing this book, and in your hands is the guide that I wished I had for my business back then.

You see, I didn't realise it at that time, but there is so much potential business opportunity when you adopt a Video Strategist mindset, and actively build your business products, services and positioning around this skill.

 BONUS MATERIAL
For downloadable worksheets and resources,
head to *engagevideomarketing.com/more*

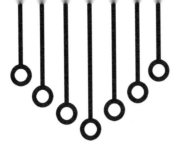

CHAPTER 2

The power of video

Video has become a dominant force online. Studies show that videos generate more engagement across every social media platform compared to images or text alone. For businesses, implementing an effective video strategy is no longer optional, it's essential for reaching and retaining customers in today's digital landscape.

Let's look at some key statistics that highlight the power of video:

- YouTube has over 2 billion monthly logged-in users who watch over 1 billion hours of video daily (Wallaroo Media, 2022).
- Facebook generates 8 billion video views every day (Meta, 2022).
- Instagram Reels get 200 billion global daily plays (Meta, 2023).
- 90% of customers say watching product videos makes them more confident in online purchase decisions (Wyzowl, 2021).

- 72% of business-to-business (B2B) buyers are more likely to purchase after watching branded videos (Wyzowl, 2021).
- Companies using video content marketing grow revenue 49% faster on average than non-video users (Wyzowl, 2021).

By the time you read this book, the above statistics will already be superseded by even more compelling data signifying our adoption of video content everywhere online.

The message is clear: video sparks engagement and drives action. For brands and businesses, implementing video into your marketing strategy is imperative. However, as we've already established, video production alone is not enough. Videos must be strategically connected to the intended audiences, business goals and desired outcomes.

Strategy is key

Simply having a YouTube channel or posting product videos on your website won't guarantee results. Effective video strategy requires identifying your target audience, understanding their pain points and motivations, defining campaign objectives, tracking measurable metrics and much more. (More on this in Part 2.)

Who do you need to reach? What message will resonate and spur them to take action? How will you distribute across platforms to gain maximum visibility? What data will determine success?

If you're an ecommerce business launching a new product line, you might create an explainer video showcasing key features and benefits. You would share this video across your company website, email marketing and social channels driving traffic, social engagement and conversions. By tracking views, click-through rates, sales conversions and ROI, you'll be able to validate the video's impact on bottom line revenue.

If you're a software company you might produce a video testimonial series featuring your clients—the goal being to build trust and credibility with potential customers during the evaluation stage. These videos would be highlighted on the pricing page of your website and shared through LinkedIn retargeting ads. With your sales team tracking lead quality, sales enquiries and customer acquisition costs, you'll be able to verify the positive influence the testimonial videos are having on your sales funnel.

The takeaway here is that videos must tie directly to your strategic business objectives and the actions you want the audience to take. Without defined goals tied to metrics, you are just posting random content hoping for a positive return.

By taking a strategic approach, you can leverage the proven power of video to captivate your audience while driving tangible results key to your business's success.

To make video work for you, you need to think beyond just production. Your role as a Video Strategist is to make informed decisions about which videos to produce and why so that your video strategy is set up for the desired success. Remember—engagement is everything. But engagement without purpose is lost opportunity. View counts mean nothing unless views translate into measurable business value.

The framework shared in the next section of this book will walk you through each of the seven elements that are essential to effective video strategy.

Your business is not different

'We sell in-person so our account reps and sales team don't need a video strategy.'

'What we do doesn't really lend itself to video marketing.'

'We're different because…'

'You see…'

'In our case…'

I've consulted to countless companies about their video strategy over the years—small, medium and large, with marketing budgets from $0 to hundreds of thousands of dollars. I've heard all the reasons why a business is different and doesn't need a video strategy or won't benefit from video marketing.

I can say with certainty that:

- Video is, and always has been, an immensely powerful communication tool.
- An online video strategy has the potential to massively impact any business, regardless of their perceived 'uniqueness' or 'specific offers'.

You see, when we break it down to root cause, every business is simply about:

- Helping someone do something
- Receiving compensation (usually in the form of money) in return.

Therefore, marketing and sales is simply the act of moving someone to do business with you.

Simple, right?

Although the nuance of execution when it comes to video marketing can change based on the business, the buyer's journey and the nature of the transaction, the underlying strategy that any business can adopt to move their ideal person to buy is the same. Core to this underlying strategy for every business are two questions:

- Who are you really selling to?
- What are you really selling?

Core question 1: Who are you really selling to?

Many businesses view their marketing and sales efforts as either business-to-consumer (B2C) or business-to-business (B2B). However, as author Chris Ducker explains in his book *Rise of the Youpreneur*, every business is ultimately about selling people-to-people (P2P).

Rather than just pushing products, effective marketing is about understanding people's needs, pains and desires. As

Ducker writes, 'Before someone becomes a *customer,* they are first and foremost a *person.*'

This P2P mindset is critical when planning video content as part of your marketing strategy. Instead of creating generic marketing videos, think about how your videos can help specific people.

Ask yourself questions like:

- Who is my ideal target audience?
- What questions or problems do they have that my product/service can solve?
- What educational or entertaining content would be valuable to them?
- What emotions do I want viewers to feel after watching my video?
- How can I tell compelling stories that relate to their lives?

By focusing on creating videos that provide value to people, rather than just promoting products and services, you are more likely to boost engagement and build lasting connections with your audience.

Videos that help people first rather than sell to them outright come across as more authentic and human. Even if your business is B2B, remember that there are actual people making purchasing decisions who have their own needs and interests.

Approaching video content creation with a P2P mindset results in marketing that is informative, relevant and meaningful.

Selling then becomes an extension of providing value rather than the sole focus. Effective video content builds trust and nurtures relationships with potential customers, rather than just shouting a message and hoping the right people will listen.

Approaching your video marketing from P2P recognises that behind every communication tactic are human beings with real problems to solve.

Lead with empathy. Aim to connect. Then help people through your videos first.

Sales won't be far behind.

Core question 2: What are you really selling?

Often in marketing, sales and business development I see businesses that are head-down focused on discovering the next growth-hacker, secret tactic that will catapult their business into the stratosphere. They're usually looking at what they deliver in their business as a 'product'; that is, something that someone will want to part with their cash to have. Whether the thing they sell is a product or a service really doesn't matter. Viewing your business as a 'product' will see you dealing in commodities.

The problem is that commodities are finite. They are transactional, and potentially limited.

A much better way to view your business is as a 'vehicle'; that is, a solution that takes a customer from where they are now, to where they want to be. Again, whether your solution is product based or a service really doesn't matter. By reframing your business in this way it dramatically changes the way you seek to market your solution.

You'll instantly change the conversation around your product or service to be about the outcome, the destination that the vehicle will be taking someone to … not just about the facts, features and rational details of the vehicle itself.

When you see your business as the solution to your customer's problem, then opportunities for growth are endless, and compelling marketing messaging is clear.

Case study—LEGO®

When LEGO® first expanded its building block sets to directly target adult hobbyists, the company struggled to gain traction. LEGO® mainly viewed these new modular building sets as a product for a B2C demographic of adult consumers. Consequently, their initial YouTube videos focused on product features and technical specifications, assuming adult builders would be drawn to the exacting details of complex builds.

The analytical, product-centred approach failed to connect with its intended audience though. Despite heavy YouTube ad spending, LEGO® saw little return in terms of site traffic or sales for its adult-focused sets. The promotional videos were essentially just commercials, videos made to serve the company, not the audience.

Realising that the demographic-based, tactical approach was not working, LEGO® made a pivotal shift. The marketing team recognised that they needed to focus less on product attributes and more on building emotional connections with people.

Rather than viewing adult fans as a monolithic demographic to sell to, they tapped into understanding the diversity of passions, interests and emotional desires tied to the LEGO® community. They developed a people-first strategy for their video marketing aimed at resonating with adult builders on a human level.

LEGO® created a documentary-style YouTube series that followed the stories of real Adult Fans of LEGO® (AFOLs). By highlighting how LEGO® building fostered friendship, creativity and community, the videos successfully appealed to adult viewers' human desires for connection, relaxation and self-expression.

One video profiled a stay-at-home dad who built LEGO® sets as a meditative escape from parental pressures, showing AFOLs bonding over their shared struggles and interests. Another video featured a Silicon Valley engineer who credited LEGO® building with helping him recover after a stroke, exemplifying how LEGO® can enable growth and achievement.

By shifting to focus on serving people's underlying emotional needs and aspirations, LEGO®'s video strategy succeeded where a myopic focus on products and tactics had failed. LEGO® was able to tap into the diversity of personalities and goals within the AFOL community by leading with real human stories over demographic data.

The people-focused video strategy also enabled LEGO® to hone in on which specific stories would best resonate with its core audience. For example, LEGO® created a full documentary spotlighting AFOLs who used LEGO® as a way to overcome adversity, exemplifying themes of resilience and pride in creation that resonated strongly.

Rather than a broad content jumble, LEGO® was strategic and selective around which people stories would truly connect emotionally and convey the empowering values of the brand. The focus was not just on viral views and clicks, but on forging authentic relationships with adult fans through shared experiences and emotions.

This intentional video strategy successfully cemented the modular building series as a hit with AFOLs. By 2021, LEGO® saw its adult fanbase grow exponentially, compelling the company to establish dedicated design teams focused entirely on adult products.

LEGO®'s journey shows that even when selling products, focusing first on understanding and serving people is key. Demographic data will only get you so far—you need to uncover the diversity of emotional motivations and values that connect us all as human beings.

LEGO® learnt that effective video marketing is not about broadcasting messages but building conversations. By listening to people's stories and crafting content to authentically resonate with them, you can foster lasting relationships beyond transactions.

They realised that video isn't just a tactic to deploy. That effective video needs to come from a place of *strategy first*.

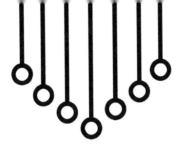

CHAPTER 3

Strategy vs Tactics

'Strategy without tactics is the slowest route to victory. Tactics without strategy is the noise before defeat.'
—Sun Tzu

The Art of War by Sun Tzu is a book that has become the backbone of everything we do both in my video agency today, and what I'm sharing with you in this book. Though written about battlefield combat, Sun Tzu's teachings have powerful application for marketing strategy today.

When we consider online video content as a marketing tactic, and the video strategy as the plan of attack, Sun Tzu perfectly captures the need for thoughtful strategy guiding skilled tactical implementation.

Having a strategic plan in place without using effective video tactics to execute will only lead to slow, incremental gains. But perhaps more dangerously, implementing a barrage of video tactics without an intentional strategy is not just expensive, but also just contributing to the overwhelming noise online.

And we already know that the digital world is a noisy place.

As Video Strategists, we must avoid adding to online noise. We need to take heed from the timeless wisdom of Sun Tzu and master the balance between strategy and tactics.

Another way to think about this is to envision the video strategy as a recipe, and individual videos and other marketing tactics as the ingredients. Simply throwing together any combination of random ingredients without a recipe will likely lead to an unpalatable mess.

With a well-designed recipe guiding you, those disparate ingredients can be creatively combined to produce a mouth-watering masterpiece. This is what an effective video strategy aims to do—provide a plan to harmonise tactical elements into something engaging and meaningful, with a harmonious outcome.

From a theoretical perspective, the importance of video strategy is clear in coordinating chaotic tactics. For business leaders, however, the ROI of video strategy must also be evident and measurable.

What is the business case for strategy?

With a strategic approach, both you and your clients can directly see the relationships between video content, target audiences, business goals and online engagement channels. There is clarity that the videos produced will be the right content, for the right people, distributed effectively to achieve defined objectives.

For example, a video strategy for an ecommerce skin care company could map out a content calendar coordinated with email campaigns and social media posts centred around promotional events and new product launches. Specific target customer segments would be defined, and video content developed to align with their preferences for tutorial and testimonial styles. Key performance indicators (KPIs) would be established, like email open rates or link click-throughs from the videos.

This strategic alignment of video tactics to business goals provides powerful proof for leaders to continue investing in video. They comprehend exactly how the videos connect to tangible desired outcomes, rather than viewing video as an intangible marketing expense.

In fact, with the right strategic insights, video becomes an investment into achieving business results, not just a cost centre. Video production budget is easier to justify when mapped clearly to metrics like increased lead generation, customer conversion rates, or brand awareness lift.

Put simply, with a video strategy in place the budget for tactically executing video makes more sense. And businesses are usually willing to pay more for video that aligns clearly to business goals.

For example, a strategic plan may call for an upfront investment in high-quality brand videos that establish thought leadership and trust. This anchors a video content library designed to reduce customer acquisition costs over time by nurturing leads through the sales funnel. The initial video investment pays dividends in lower marketing costs and faster sales down the road.

Conversely, a reactive approach to video without strategic underpinning can lead to wasteful spending. Well-intentioned but disjointed marketing tactics fail to compound effects and end up providing minimal ROI.

Think of a clothing brand quickly producing a new collection of social videos each week because they heard 'video is hot right now.' With no overarching strategy, this tactical scramble often leads to 'vanity metrics' showing spikes of views or follows without sustainable growth. But key business metrics such as website traffic and sales remain unchanged as video efforts flop without a solid foundation.

This is why Sun Tzu's teachings hold true centuries later. While the marketing battlefield today may seem far removed from ancient combat, success still depends on coordinating strategy and tactics.

Video production alone is not enough. But a strong video strategy empowers those tactical elements to effectively work together to achieve business success. It provides a recipe for video content that speaks to the motivations of your customers, coordinated across platforms to nurture their journey from prospect to evangelist.

With strategic guidance, video becomes not just a communications medium but also a catalyst for measurable business growth.

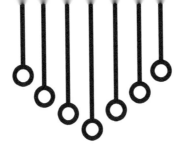

CHAPTER 4

The danger of video for video's sake

Something I see a lot in my line of work is businesses who decide to make a video because it seems like a good idea, but without much strategic thought. (I call this the 'form approach'.) Maybe someone suggested it, or they saw viral videos and thought they should jump on the bandwagon too. Or they know their target audience loves video, so they leap right into production.

Once the video is made, they post it online, get some vanity metrics like view counts, congratulate themselves, and don't think deeply about it until the next time someone says 'let's do another video!'

This 'video for video's sake' methodology is problematic. It leads to disjointed efforts that fail to deliver meaningful business impact.

A much better mindset is a strategic approach to video. When you take this approach the first questions are focused on core business goals and target audience needs:

- What key metric do we need to improve? (Website visits, online sales, etc.)
- How can video help address this goal?
- Who are we trying to reach and influence?
- What content would uniquely appeal to them?

Only after this strategic foundation is laid does production begin. There is clarity on the types of videos that have the highest likelihood of achieving the intended outcome.

With the strategic approach, video production is just one piece of a comprehensive process:

1. Identify business goal and metrics to improve.
2. Determine if video is the right medium to drive impact.
3. Research target audience motivations and video preferences.
4. Develop intentionally-designed video content optimised for goals.
5. Implement video distribution and promotion strategy.
6. Analyse performance data and optimise approach.

This creates an aligned, results-driven use of video. Content is crafted to speak directly to the target audience and move them towards the desired action.

Let's compare the differences between the form and strategic approaches:

Form approach	Strategic approach
1. Decide to make a video because it seems like a good idea.	1. Identify key business goal first and determine if video can drive impact.
2. Create generic video focused on company and products.	2. Research target audience needs and motivations to shape content.
3. Post video and track basic view metrics.	3. Map out video production and distribution strategy.
4. Create next video reactively when stakeholders suggest it.	4. Analyse performance and refine approach to optimise business results.

With the strategic methodology, there is a tight linkage between the videos produced and their intended outcomes. Video becomes a purposeful tool, not just something to check off a marketing list.

Example—Ecommerce company

Let's take the example of an ecommerce company who needs to increase sales of their new product line. Research shows their target buyers respond well to unboxing and review formats.

The **form approach** might entail a generic brand video about the product launch that briefly shows the new items. It gets posted on social media without much promotion or targeting. The only metric tracked is overall post likes or views.

Conversely, the **strategic approach** would involve partnering with relevant influencers to produce customised unboxing videos centred around use cases relevant to those buyers. These would be distributed through organic social media and via paid ads targeting that audience segment.

Performance data like sales or lead generation for the specific product line would measure impact. The approach gets refined based on what content and distribution tactics demonstrate the highest ROI.

The business impact between these two approaches is night and day. One seeds the internet with trusted content deliberately designed to get buyers excited and drive sales. The other is essentially just wasted creative effort.

Video for video's sake is no longer enough in today's crowded online space. Focus first on strategic alignment to business goals and audience needs. Let this guide your creative process. Embrace video as part of a coordinated plan, not just a standalone tactic.

This amplifies the power of video to educate, connect emotionally and motivate action. It enables you to stand out from the noisy crowd and achieve measurable results. Video becomes a driving force when backed by strategy.

BONUS MATERIAL

For downloadable worksheets and resources, head to *engagevideomarketing.com/more*

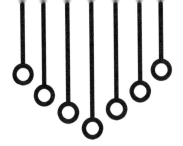

CHAPTER 5

You don't actually want a video

There's an old marketing maxim that says people don't want a quarter-inch drill bit, they want a quarter-inch hole.

This adage highlights that customers aren't interested in a product for its own sake—they want the solution it provides. The drill bit has no inherent value; it's the hole it can drill that delivers utility.

But we can take this even further. Do people really just want a generic hole in the wall? Not at all. They want that hole so they can insert a screw to hang up a shelf. And they probably don't care much about the shelf itself either. The shelf creates storage space where they can finally display that framed photo of their late grandfather, which provides a heartwarming reminder of beloved family memories.

The displaying of that photo, and the emotions it evokes, is the real goal. Not the drill, not the hole, not even the shelf—those are all just means to an end.

This principle very much applies to businesses seeking out video production too. Clients may think they want a video, but what they're really after are **the results an effective video strategy can deliver.**

As a video producer, it's critical to recognise your clients aren't coming to you for the video itself. They want what that video can potentially do for their business—raise brand awareness, increase sales, generate more leads, etc.

Don't make the mistake of simply focusing on **video creation.** You must position yourself as **selling the solution,** with video as the vehicle to get them there. Ask probing questions to understand the client's true underlying goals and how video can achieve them.

For business owners and marketers, apply this same lens when considering investing in custom video production. Avoid seeking video for its own sake without tying it to strategic objectives. Get clear on the specific business outcomes you're aiming for and how original video content could drive measurable impact.

Consider the difference between how a generic video producer versus a Video Strategist approaches a lead generation campaign.

The producer's focus is on output metrics—producing high quality video content within time and budget. The client pays a set commodity rate based on production factors like filming hours and editing complexity. It's centred around tactics first.

Conversely, the strategist first helps the client define campaign goals and quantifiable KPIs, like increasing qualified leads by 25% quarter-over-quarter. The video concept and production approach are designed intentionally to drive that specific outcome.

Pricing is value-based, factoring in the potential revenue lift generated for the client by the video strategy. The focus is on achieving the desired solution and outcome.

For the client, the difference comes down to investing in a fixed-cost, one-off branded video asset versus a flexible, value-based video marketing strategy that ties directly to revenue growth. One is a tactical support for the marketing machine, while the other becomes the strategic fuel that drives it forward.

Let's say the target customer persona responds well to educational content and testimonials. The strategist may propose an ongoing series of 'day in the life' videos showcasing clients using the product effectively.

These authentic stories educate prospects similarly situated to those featured clients, nurturing them towards a lead conversion. The videos are distributed through targeted social ads and email campaigns coordinated with sales outreach.

Performance metrics then inform an agile content optimisation loop. The approach evolves based on which video styles, calls to action and distribution channels prove most effective for the client's goals.

This kind of solution-focused process ensures video production has a clear purpose beyond just creating branded content. There is tangible linkage between views and results.

So for both video producers and business owners, remember— it's not about the video. You ultimately want what that video can achieve. Whether it's increased sales, lower cost per lead or greater brand loyalty, the business objectives matter most.

Your value as a Video Strategist is in helping clients (or your own business) to first define those tangible goals for video, then mapping out an intentional strategy to get there. Let content creation flow from that solid strategic foundation.

Sell the hole, not the drill bit. Put the solution and outcome first, videos second. This approach makes video marketing something that fuels business growth, not just supports a checked-box tactic.

BONUS MATERIAL

For downloadable worksheets and resources,
head to *engagevideomarketing.com/more*

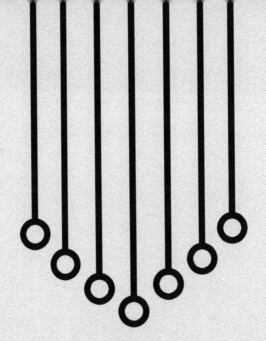

PART 2

The 7 Elements of Video Strategy

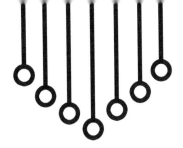

CHAPTER 6

The Strategic Content Planning Process

If you want to succeed with online video marketing, there are seven elements of video strategy you need to be aware of, and seven corresponding steps that must be followed. Get these key elements and associated steps right, and your video content will be set up for maximum engagement and results. Neglect any of them, and your efforts risk falling flat.

Here's what the strategic content planning process should look like.

Step 1: Understand the Audience

First and foremost, you need to understand your audience. This means knowing what motivates them, what their pain points are, and what will drive them to engage with your content and take action. Conduct thorough audience research, analyse demographic data, and gather insights from customer feedback to build a clear picture of your target audience.

We will cover this in Chapter 7.

Step 2: Identify the Goal

Each video should have a clear, defined goal. Are you aiming to increase brand positioning, generate social engagement, drive sales or increase customer delight? Identifying the intended goal for the video ensures that every piece of content you produce serves a specific purpose and contributes to your broader marketing objectives.

Chapter 8 will cover this in detail.

Step 3: Brainstorm and decide on the Content

Once you understand your audience and have identified the goal, it's time to brainstorm content ideas. Focus on what you want to communicate to your audience and how you'll position your message. This involves deciding on the key messages you want to convey, the tone and style of the video, and the type of content that will best resonate with your audience.

This will be the topic of Chapter 9.

Step 4: Consider Distribution channels

Think about where your video will be distributed as the channels you use will signficantly impact the production and format of your video. For example, videos for social media might need to be shorter and more engaging, while videos for your website can be longer and more detailed. Understanding the nuances of each platform will help you optimise your content for maximum reach and engagement.

Stay tuned for Chapter 10 when we dive deeper into distribution.

Step 5: Plan for Optimisation

Optimisation is essential for ensuring that your video reaches the right audience and performs well. This involves considering Search Engine Optimisation (SEO) best practices, using relevant keywords, and optimising video titles, descriptions and tags. It also means thinking about how to encourage engagement through calls to action and interactive elements.

We'll go deeper with optimisation in Chapter 11.

Step 6: Measure Success

How will you measure the success of your video? This could involve tracking metrics such as views, engagement rates, click-through rates, conversions and overall ROI. Having clear metrics in place allows you to evaluate the effectiveness of your video and make data-driven decisions for future content.

Those metrics will be unveiled in Chapter 12.

Step 7: Design the Production

Finally, design the production of the video to suit all the considerations above. This includes planning the script, storyboard, filming, editing and post-production processes. Ensure that every element of the production aligns with your strategic goals and resonates with your audience.

Chapter 13 has the production side outlined in more detail.

The order of the seven elements is very deliberate. Each one feeds into the next in a way that builds a cohesive, effective framework:

Audience → Goals → Content → Distribution
→ Optimisation → Metrics → Production

It's important to recognise these aren't just isolated factors. The interconnected flow is what matters. When all seven are addressed strategically in this way, you end up with video content that resonates at every step of the customer journey. Your videos will be:

- The right content
- For the right people
- Distributed and promoted in the right way

- Optimised for discoverability
- Tracked with the right metrics
- Produced in a style that fits your strategic objectives.

Now that you have a high-level view of the seven elements, let's explore each one in depth.

BONUS MATERIAL

For downloadable worksheets and resources, head to *engagevideomarketing.com/more*

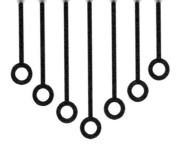

CHAPTER 7

Audience

When we understand and respect the fact that business is all about serving others, not our own interests, we can quickly connect the fact that our audience, (our target market, our customers and our community) are the most important element to consider in a marketing strategy.

I know for some of you this may seem obvious, or a no-brainer. But I have to keep harping on about it because so many businesses I come across are creating content to serve their own needs first ahead of the needs of their target customer.

Remember, in its simplest form marketing is about moving people to take action. If we don't know who the PEOPLE are that we are trying to MOVE, then we simply can't be effective with our marketing.

As Video Strategists we need to start our process by understanding the company's ideal audience. And one of the most effective ways to do this is by defining clear and detailed customer avatars.

I know, you've probably heard that marketing buzzword a bunch of times. But it really does continue to surprise me how many businesses I talk to who still don't have clarity on their audience or who their ideal customers actually are.

Customer avatars

Developing customer avatars is a fine mix between data and creativity. The best way to approach this is to base your thoughts on facts, but allow your creativity and imagination to fill out the 'shadows'.

Defining a customer avatar requires three key areas:

- Demographics
- Psychographics
- Behaviours.

It is critical to be really specific in this process and building out the profile of one particular imaginary or 'real' customer, not a generic, demographic group.

Let's take a look at a template you can use to define a concise customer avatar for your business or your clients.

Demographics	
Name	
Age	
Gender	
Location	
Role/position	
Key Features	
Psychographics	
Goals	
Challenges	
Objections	
Behaviour Profile	
What they do	
Where they go	
Triggers	
Key Message	

This multi-section document provides a framework to compile extensive details on demographics, psychographics, behaviours, pain points and desired messaging that describe your perfect customer persona. Let's dive deeper into each part.

1. Demographics

This section covers basic attributes like age, gender, location, and professional role or job title. While you may be targeting a broad market segment, identifying specific demographic details puts a tangible face to that audience.

For example, instead of 'working professionals', you could identify a 32-year-old female sales manager in Melbourne. This allows the potentially intangible, to begin to be perceived in the 'real world'.

2. Psychographics

Details here reveal the inner world of your audience including goals, challenges and objections. What aspirations do they have professionally or personally? What difficulties are they experiencing in relation to your industry or offerings? Where might there be hesitation or convincing needed?

Perhaps career advancement is a major goal but the time commitment of extra training is a hurdle. Uncovering these insights breathes life into the factual demographics and begins to inform critical messaging angles that are a powerhouse for your marketing.

3. Behaviour profile

This focuses on relevant actions and behaviours of your audience. What do they already do related to your field? Where do they spend time online and offline? What motivates purchases or product/service selection?

Understanding your audience's habits, environments and triggers paints a full behavioural picture, and serves as a foundation to understanding their entire customer journey.

4. Key message

Given your audience avatar's attributes, goals and behaviours, what messaging do they need to hear from you to become a customer? This section prompts you to distill what video content must communicate, and how it should be perceived by the intended audience in order to resonate and compel action.

The message should align closely with the psychographics and behavioural profile of that particular persona. Speak directly to their established needs and motivations.

Compiling these details brings your audience avatar to life as an actual person rather than a vague demographic segment. It becomes easy to envision creating videos that speak to their unique needs.

Example audience avatar #1 Mortgage Broker

ABC Mortgage Brokers helps connect people with the best home loans for their needs. One of their core target audiences is first-time home buyers.

Here is a detailed avatar created for this audience segment:

First-time Fiona is a 28-year-old first-time homebuyer searching for her first mortgage. She works as a high school teacher in the suburbs of Detroit and is hoping to buy a small condo in the city. However, she has student debt from college and is unsure of how much she can afford. Fiona gets most of her information online but finds the mortgage process overwhelming. She needs guidance matching her budget to the right mortgage products.

Audience Avatar: First-Time Fiona (First-time Homebuyer)

Demographics	
Name	Fiona
Age	28
Gender	Female
Location	Detroit suburbs
Role/position	High school teacher
Key Features	First-time homebuyer, looking to purchase condo in city
Psychographics	
Goals	Buy first home (condo) in Detroit
Challenges	Student debt, unsure how much is affordable, overwhelmed by mortgage options
Objections	Fear of spending too much on a house and being house poor
Behaviour Profile	
What they do	Research mortgages and down payment info online, talks to friends/family for advice
Where they go	Zillow, real estate sites, mortgage calculators
Triggers	Wants more space than current rental, ready to stop paying landlord
Key Message	
We understand first-time homebuyers and make mortgages simple. Our expertise matches you with the perfect loan for your budget and life.	

Example audience avatar #2
Handmade Jewellery Ecommerce Store

Handcrafted Jewellery Co. is an online retailer selling artisan-made necklaces, earrings, rings and bracelets. A key audience is traditional jewellery buyers who shop in-store and at markets but have never purchased online.

Below is a detailed avatar created for this audience segment:

Hesitant Heather is a 45-year-old mother of two who lives in the Denver suburbs. She loves supporting local artists and handmade crafts. Heather frequently shops for jewellery at weekend markets, boutiques and craft fairs. However, she has concerns about the online experience and security. She needs reassurance that buying handmade pieces virtually can be just as lovely.

Audience Avatar: Hesitant Heather (Traditional Jewellery Buyer)

Demographics	
Name	Heather
Age	45
Gender	Female
Location	Littleton, Colorado (Denver suburb)
Role/position	Stay-at-home parent with two kids (ages 8 and 12)
Key Features	Enjoys handmade jewellery, used to in-person shopping at markets/boutiques

Psychographics	
Goals	Find unique handcrafted jewellery that expresses her personal style. Support small/local artists. Buy pieces that can be handed down.
Challenges	Unsure about spending $100-$300 on jewellery without seeing it first. Concerns over sizing, security and return process buying online.
Objections	Loves the experience of boutique shopping. Worried online lacks ability to inspect jewellery closely or get expert recommendations. Doesn't trust photos to capture details fully.
Behaviour Profile	
What they do	Shops at local craft fairs and farmers' markets. Visits boutiques in trendy neighbourhoods. Browses Etsy but rarely purchases. Goes to art galleries and museums.
Where they go	Littleton Farmers Market, Renegade Craft Fair, boutiques on Tennyson St., museums for inspiration. Etsy to browse.
Triggers	Handcrafted, customised touches like carved gems or delicate filigree. Supporting small businesses and artists.
Key Message	

Our online shop recaptures the wonder of boutique jewellery shopping—you can discover one-of-a-kind handmade treasures, connect with our artists, and find pieces as lovely as anything in your favourite stores. Our 'Artisan Assurance: Your Perfect Piece or Your Money Back!' return and refund policy makes buying online risk-free.

Note that in the above two examples, the first one is quite simple and only scratches the surface. The second example shows a more detailed response, and is the preferred approach to take where time and information allow.

For many businesses you're going to likely have multiple customer avatars that need to be developed. However, it's important not to go too broad, too wide or have too many avatars in which any business is attempting to market and sell to. Focus down, be clear on who your ideal target audience is and how you want to 'show up' for them.

My suggestion—keep your avatars to two or perhaps three key people you are trying to reach.

- -

Audience Avatar—Pro Tips

Pro Tip 1: Give your avatar a name

Coming up with a specific name like 'Agency Anna' or 'Styling Simon' makes your avatar a concrete person rather than a generic demographic. While naming may come later, the right name can really bring your avatar to life in your mind when creating content.

I'm also a big fan of using alliteration and descriptive adjectives along with the avatar name to make them more memorable and identifiable in a business.

Pro Tip 2: Be as specific as possible

Your avatar should represent one highly detailed person, not a wide range of people. Jennifer is a 32-year-old social media manager in Balmoral, Sydney, not a 'millennial professional'. Vivid specificity is key.

Pro Tip 3: Base your avatar on existing ideal customers when possible

Looking at sales data and analytics for current best customers and profiling common patterns makes populating avatar details easier. Basing Jennifer on your top social media client from Sydney gives you real insights to work from.

Pro Tip 4: Don't obsess over perfecting the language as you draft

Get the details down first, even if rough. You can always refine the wording later after fleshing out the meaty content. Don't let perfectionism trip you up initially.

Pro Tip 5: Adapt any template sections needed to suit your business or service

If a generic location field isn't as relevant, customise your avatar template to capture attributes that are key. Shape the framework around your audience.

Once we're clear on who we're trying to influence with our video strategy, and we've built out a detailed understanding of who they are, their pain, their desires and their behaviours online, we're better placed to move forward towards a highly effective video strategy.

The next section in this chapter will take this understanding and apply it to something called the customer journey. This understanding was the real game changer in my business.

Customer journey

In the previous section you detailed the customer avatars that you're marketing to. Now it's time to analyse the journey the customer will go on before they eventually decide to buy from a business. This journey is called the customer journey.

Understanding how people buy, their motivations, needs and actions mean we can be so much more effective in creating the right video content and using it in the right way to move our audience to action.

The cool thing about the customer journey is that it's directly related to human nature—it's ingrained in all of us. As Video Strategists, when we harness this understanding it's kind of like a marketing superpower—one that your clients are going to love you for.

Whether we're buying a doughnut as we walk through the local shopping mall or deciding which law firm to work with on a complicated legal matter we all go through the same overarching buyer journey. Which, in the simplest terms is:

Feel pain → Seek solutions → Decide on solution

If we were to translate the above into phases, this is what it would look like:

Awareness → Consideration → Purchase

Buyers will move at their own pace, or the pace at which we encourage them to move, from left to right. That is:

- From awareness of a need

- Through consideration of their options
- Then eventually to a purchase/conversion/sale.

As the customer moves through this journey, their needs change. As their needs change, the way we as marketers need to communicate with them also changes.

Something that's important to understand here is that people buy with *emotion* and then justify that decision with *logic*. To that end, before we dive into the phases of the customer journey, it's important to first understand the human brain a little better.

The human brain and video marketing

Understanding even just basic brain science can radically shift how we can approach crafting marketing strategies and campaigns, especially when leveraging a powerful medium like video.

So let's take a look under the hood at the triune brain model to better grasp exactly how our grey matter impacts the customer journey.

The triune brain model

While somewhat simplified, the triune brain model proposes that the human brain developed through three distinct evolutionary stages, each building upon the last:

The Reptilian Brain (Basal Ganglia)

The oldest part of our brain, stemming back to prehistoric

times. This portion controls core bodily functions required for basic survival—breathing, heartbeat, reflexes. Decision-making is rooted at the most primal level of gut instinct.

The Limbic System

This area of the brain evolved alongside the emotional capacities of mammals. It includes the amygdala, hippocampus and other structures governing feelings, memories, attention and emotional responses. The limbic system plays a key role in determining our value judgments on whether to trust or invest deeply in something.

The Neocortex

The outermost layer, and the key distinction for modern humans and primates. Here we find the centres for higher order thinking—language, logic, reasoning, consciousness and abstract thought. It's the rational, calculating brain at work.

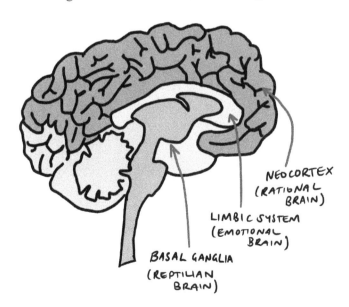

NEOCORTEX (RATIONAL BRAIN)

LIMBIC SYSTEM (EMOTIONAL BRAIN)

BASAL GANGLIA (REPTILIAN BRAIN)

Note: While the triune brain theory has been largely discredited by contemporary neuroscience—which understands brain function as more interconnected and less hierarchical—it remains a valuable conceptual model for understanding psychological and marketing dynamics.

So how exactly does understanding this triune brain structure help us better connect through video marketing?

The limits of logic

As marketers, our goal is to convince people to buy, right? So, usually a default approach is to focus our marketing messaging around communicating the features, benefits and all the amazing bells and whistles that our product or solution can provide to a customer.

After all, if we can get all the important information across then surely someone will be ready to buy—right?

Brain imaging studies highlight the key flaw in this approach. The rational neocortex actually places immense cognitive load on the brain. It takes intense energy and processing power to interpret complex information through this rational filter.

Research from scholars like Stanford's Baba Shiv demonstrates just how little willpower the logical brain actually has. In one study[1], Shiv had participants who had completed a memory task choose between chocolate cake (unhealthy but appealing) or fruit salad (healthy but unexciting).

---

1   Heart and Mind in Conflict: The Interplay of Affect and Cognition in Consumer Decision Making, Baba Shiv and Alexander Fedorikhin Journal of Consumer Research, 1999

Those trying to memorise a longer sequence of numbers were 21% more likely to cave and indulge in the cake compared to those only memorising 1-2 digits. Even mild cognitive load drastically impaired rational decision making when pitted against primal desire.

The implication is clear—if marketing approaches lead by bombarding people with stats, specs and dry facts, our logical brains quickly become overwhelmed. We simply do not have the mental resources to process it all rationally, especially amidst a sea of other daily distractions.

Our overtaxed brains simply cannot resist deferring to the limbic system's primal instincts and impulses instead. So as marketers, before we can even convey our well-reasoned value props, audiences have already made snap judgments on their overall emotional resonance.

Cracking the emotional code

Compared to the neocortex, the limbic system processes data much more rapidly and automatically through emotion. Within fractions of a second, our deep limbic pathways can deem whether something appears desirable, trustworthy or threatening.

In fact, this primitive brain conducts nearly all initial evaluations by rapidly processing non-verbal sensory inputs like sights, sounds and smells, NOT through rational consideration of facts. These first impressions are pivotal, as emotional impact creates lingering memorability or lack thereof.

We feel before we think on a rational level.

How video engages each part of the brain

This is precisely where thoughtfully produced video content can make all the difference in our marketing efforts. While text-based ads or sales pages may fall flat, well-crafted video possesses the unique ability to more holistically engage all three 'brains':

For the Reptilian Brain:

- Sights, sounds and motion tap into raw senses.
- Faces, colours and aesthetics convey immediate 'friend or foe' signals.
- Pacing and editing induce desired physiological responses.

For the Limbic Brain:

- Emotionally resonant storytelling and authentic tone builds trust.
- Music and voice transcend language barriers triggering nostalgia, aspirations or met needs.

For the Neocortex:

- Tailored messaging educates and informs.
- Clear comprehension of information overcomes rational objections.

Crafted strategically, videos can bypass neocortex overload by tapping into the full spectrum of human experience. They foster instantaneous emotional connections that prime ideal conditions for rational consideration and purchase.

The customer journey is like dating

A great way to think about the customer journey, and how it works in an intensely human way is to liken it to dating.

Consider that first date. You're at the **awareness stage** of that journey and as such we understand the importance of dressing nice, smiling, making eye contact, telling stories and perhaps even making them laugh. We're doing things to get them to connect with us on an emotional level. We are hoping to provide a good first impression as we understand it's so critical in getting to that next stage, and further dates.

And, if we've successfully connected on the right emotional level with our date then we move to the **consideration stage**. This is where we need to continue to connect emotionally but some rational decision-making starts coming in to play. Our date is now wanting to learn more about who we really are, they want to feel informed, understand that they can trust us, that we fit with what they're really looking for in a partner and so on.

So, if we've done a good job here and everything's going well then the relationship moves to the final stage—**the sale**.

Now I'll let you work out on your own what the 'sale' is in my dating analogy, however let's just say that if we go straight for that outcome, you'll usually end up with a slap in the face.

Unfortunately, for so many in marketing and sales that's exactly what they tend to do. They go straight for the sale, without respecting the customer's journey and spending time building the right relationships first.

The phases of the customer journey

Let's consider what's actually going through the heads of our customer as they move through the various phases to purchase.

1. Awareness

At the awareness phase of the customer journey a potential client or prospect is predominantly dealing with their own emotion (limbic system). That is, the emotional connection they feel about the problem they have that will (potentially) lead them to buy from you.

This emotion could be a negative emotion, a pain point, or even a positive feeling—perhaps excitement or anticipation of what's to come. At the awareness phase a customer isn't thinking about who can solve their problem, or even rationalising what their problem really is!

They're all about 'what's in it for me!' and when we understand this—the importance of communicating to the target audience with their needs, desires and emotional state in mind becomes really clear.

What we're aiming to achieve in this first awareness phase is to connect on the right emotional level with our audience. To get them to **'buy-in' to our brand** well before we ask them to **buy from our brand**.

We need to assume here that the audience is 'cold', that is, has never heard of our brand before and through this first phase we want them to sit up and pay attention. To connect emotionally with what we are all about, and start them on the road to feeling that we are the right fit for their needs.

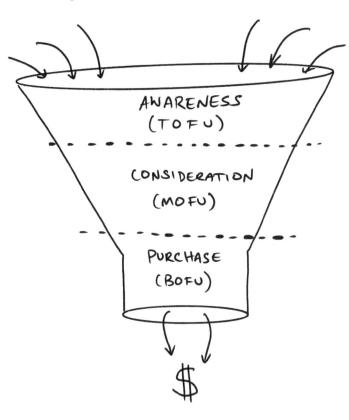

In marketing terms the customer journey is often represented as a funnel. The awareness phase is at the top of the funnel (sometimes shortened and referred to as TOFU) and here the potential audience size is considerably larger, but as an audience moves through to purchase the audience size gets smaller and much more ready to buy. At the awareness phase we're all about getting people into the funnel, and the best way to do this is to appeal to an audience's emotions—recognising that emotions are what drives every purchase decision from the outset.

Do this right, and the customer will be positively 'aware' of our brand, and ready to engage further on the journey to potentially buy from us.

2. Consideration

At the consideration phase (middle of the funnel, or MOFU) an audience is interested in potentially purchasing but is not yet sure who to buy from, or even if they will be buying. As such, they are seeking to engage further, to learn more, to have their questions answered and seek out the right fit for their needs. Emotions are certainly still at play here but rational decision-making is starting to become apparent. They've potentially bought in to your brand, but are you actually the right fit, can you deliver on the promises you've made and can you actually help them?

The goal here, therefore, is to educate, entertain or inspire. You want to provide value to your audience but without the direct expectation that they buy from you.

Do this well, and you'll move the right portion of the target audience further down the customer journey funnel into the final phase—'purchase'.

3. Purchase

As we move towards the purchase (bottom of the funnel, or BOFU) human nature continues to play a part, as now our target audience's rational (neocortex) brain takes control. Emotions are somewhat set aside as now it's all about the facts and figures.

The audience is saying to themselves:

> *'Okay, I get what you're about and think you're awesome. I also feel that I can trust you, and you are a good fit for me. But can you actually deliver? And what's the process of buying from you, working with you, or using your product actually like? Am I actually making the right decision here?'*

Recognising where your audience is at during this phase, we can understand that our goal is to answer those lingering questions. To allay any final concerns a potential customer may have and to get them across the line to buy. By providing rational information in a strategic and human centred way we'll be able to move the audience effectively through to a sale.

A fourth phase—advocacy

Now—there is one more phase to consider here in the customer journey. It's the one where a customer is following a sale. In the perfect world, we now consider them in the 'advocacy' stage of their journey. That is, they've bought from us, and now we want to encourage them to buy again, or tell others about us in order to further increase brand awareness and engagement. In the advocacy stage it's all about maintaining positive brand connections, and providing content that empowers an advocate to stay connected, consider future purchasing and to share their experiences with the brand.

When we think back to our dating analogy, this advocacy stage is what fuels a long-term successful relationship. Where it's no longer purely 'transactional' but mutually beneficial.

In fact, if we consider the customer journey in this way we can imagine that it isn't really a linear journey but rather a circular one. Where advocates drive new awareness to the top of the funnel and the journey begins again.

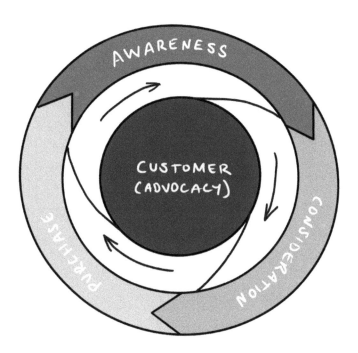

Customer research

Developing a customer avatar gives us a clear idea of who we're trying to communicate to and therefore influence with our video strategy.

Understanding the customer journey means we know how human brains work and how humans make decisions to buy.

The next step is to do customer research to give us data to assist with sound decision-making as Video Strategists. It's been said that data never lies, and this couldn't be more true for a video strategy.

There are three main customer research strategies I'll break down in this chapter:

1. Audience surveys
2. Keyword research and trend analysis
3. Empathy mapping.

There are also some significant insights into your audience to be gained by analysing the data provided by any of your video distribution channels, however we'll be diving deeper into those metrics in Chapter 12 so we'll save that until then.

1. Audience surveys

This is a simple customer research strategy that is severely underutilised in digital marketing.

By using online survey tools such as SurveyMonkey or Typeform, or even simple single question polls in YouTube cards, live videos, Facebook updates or Instagram stories you can gather valuable data about your audience that you might otherwise not have had at your disposal.

Audience Survey Tips

When designing surveys for audience research, you need to be conscious that people are time-poor and will often focus on the first couple of questions more than the rest.

For this reason, I recommend an open question along the lines of the below to start:

What's the one thing you struggle with most when it comes to XXX?

(Where XXX is the thing you help your audience with.)

The idea here is that in the very first response you'll gain valuable information about the biggest pain points right now for your customers. By giving them room to answer the question with as little or as much information as they want, you'll get responses ranging from one or two word answers right up to multiple paragraph rants. When you collate this data along with the other responses in your survey you gain a really powerful view into how your audience ticks, and what language they use around the problems that they are feeling.

---

2. Keyword research and trend analysis

The next customer research strategy you can deploy is some simple keyword research. By tapping into the available data from search engines such as Google, we'll get insights into:

- What our audience is searching for online
- What words they are using in search engines
- How likely certain search terms are to come up in results.

The insights we get here will allow us to better understand our potential audience's online behaviour, and the language they're using when seeking out products or services such as ours. The keyword research will also provide us with content ideas and potentially uncover previously unthought of areas in which to focus our video strategy for maximum effect.

This keyword research is also the backbone of the 'optimisation' element we'll take a deeper look at in Chapter 11.

When it comes to keyword research, my go-to tools are:

- Google Keyword Planner
- YouTube/Google Search's search suggestions.

Keyword Planner

Google Keyword Planner is a powerful tool originally designed for advertisers to research keywords for their Google Ads campaigns. However, its functionality extends far beyond paid advertising. For Video Strategists, Keyword Planner is an invaluable resource for understanding what audiences are searching for, helping to tailor video content to meet these interests and needs.

Quick guide to using Keyword Planner for customer research

To use Keyword Planner, you'll need a Google Ads account. Once logged in to that account, access the Keyword Planner under the 'Tools and Settings' menu. Here, you have two primary options: 'Discover new keywords' and 'Get search volume and forecasts'. For audience research, 'Discover new keywords' is most pertinent.

How to research keywords relevant to your audience

1. Enter products or services

Begin by entering terms related to your product or

service. For example, if you're creating videos for a fitness brand, you might start with terms like 'workout routines', 'fitness tips', and 'home exercise'.

2. Refine your search

Use filters to narrow down your audience by location, language, and search networks. This helps in identifying the most relevant keywords for your specific audience.

3. Analyze keyword ideas

Keyword Planner will provide a list of related keywords, along with useful data such as average monthly searches, competition level, and top of page bid range. This information helps gauge the popularity and competitiveness of each keyword.

Example: Fitness Brand Video Strategy

Keyword ideas: For 'workout routines', you might find related keywords like 'beginner home workouts' or 'short fitness routines'.

Search volume: High search volume for 'home exercise tips' indicates a strong interest in this area.

Competition: If competition is high for certain keywords, it might be an indication of a saturated market.

Using the insights from Keyword Planner

Here are three areas where you can put the insights you gain from your customer research in Keyword Planner to good work:

1. **Content ideas:** Keywords with high search volumes can inspire topics for your videos. If 'yoga for beginners' has a high search volume, creating a video series on this topic might attract a large audience.

2. **SEO optimisation:** Use these keywords in your video titles, descriptions, and tags to improve SEO which translates to increased visibility on Google and YouTube.

3. **Understanding trends:** Seasonal trends in keyword searches can guide the timing of your video releases.

Google Keyword Planner is more than just a tool for advertisers. It's a window into the interests and needs of your potential audience. By strategically using this tool, you can align your video content with what your audience is actively searching for, increasing engagement and reach.

YouTube/Google Search's search suggestions

YouTube and Google Search's search suggestions are often overlooked but are incredibly useful for understanding audience interests and queries. These suggestions, generated based on popular searches, offer real-time insights into what people are looking for.

Quick guide to using Search Suggestions

1. Start typing a query

Go to YouTube or Google and start typing a query related to your field. For instance, if you're making videos about cooking, start with 'how to cook'.

2. Analyse the suggestions

Pay attention to the suggestions that appear. These are based on common searches and represent what people are interested in.

3. Dive deeper

Choose a suggestion and then add additional letters or words to refine and explore deeper queries.

Example: Cooking Channel Video Strategy

Initial suggestions: Typing 'how to cook' might bring up suggestions like 'how to cook rice', 'how to cook pasta' or 'how to cook healthy meals on a budget'.

Refined search: Adding 'for beginners' might show 'how to cook for beginners guide' or 'easy cooking tips for beginners'.

Using the insights from search suggestions

Here are three areas where you can put the insights you gain from search suggestions to work:

1. **Content creation:** These suggestions can guide the creation of targeted videos. If "easy cooking tips for

beginners" is a common search, a video series catering to novice cooks could be very effective.

2. **Understanding audience language:** The way people phrase their searches can guide the language you use in your video titles and descriptions, making them more relatable and searchable.

3. **Identifying niche topics:** Sometimes, these suggestions can reveal niche topics that haven't been extensively covered, providing an opportunity to create unique content.

Advantages of using YouTube/Google Search's search suggestions

There are three key advantages to using search suggestions:

1. **Cost-effective research:** Unlike paid tools, this method of audience research is free and easy to use.

2. **Real-time insights:** Suggestions are updated in real-time, reflecting current trends and interests.

3. **Direct connection to audience needs:** These searches directly reflect the queries and interests of your potential audience.

Pro Tips for YouTube/ Google Search's search suggestions

Boolean search techniques offer advanced methods for refining search queries, allowing Video Strategists to delve deeper into audience interests and preferences.

Using Quotation Marks (" ")

Quotation marks are employed to search for an exact phrase, ensuring the search results contain that specific string of words.

Example: *Searching for "quick dinner recipes" (in quotes) will yield suggestions specifically containing this phrase, which can be invaluable for a cooking channel seeking to target this exact query.*

Use of Underscores (_)

Underscores act as placeholders for unknown or variable words in a search query. They can be used not just at the end of a phrase but also in the middle or at the beginning.

Example: *A search like "how to cook _ chicken" can reveal various cooking methods or recipes related to chicken (eg: "how to cook free range chicken", or "how to cook fried chicken", whereas "_ quick meals" might uncover different types of quick meals people are searching for such as "healthy quick meals" or "keto quick meals".)*

Bonus tips for underscores

- **Positional flexibility:** Experiment with placing the underscore at different points in your query to explore a range of topics and questions.

- **Uncover diverse interests:** Using underscores in various positions can help in identifying a wide array of audience interests and content gaps.

Utilising the Plus (+) and Minus (-) Signs

The plus and minus signs are used to include or exclude specific words in your search results.

- **Plus Sign (+):** Ensures that the included term must be in the search results. For example, "healthy+salads" will only show suggestions where 'salads' is a definite part of the search.

- **Minus Sign (-):** Excludes certain words from your search results. For instance, "baking -sugar" can be used to find suggestions related to sugar-free baking.

Use of the OR operator

The OR operator is used to search for multiple terms simultaneously, broadening the scope of your research.

Example: A search like "high protein OR low carb meals" can give you a broader range of dietary meal suggestions, useful for a nutrition-focused channel.

YouTube and Google Search's search suggestions are simple yet powerful tools for gauging audience interest. By tapping into the wealth of data these suggestions provide, Video Strategists can create content that not only resonates with their audience but also addresses their specific queries and needs. This approach ensures that your video content is both relevant and sought-after, positioning it for greater visibility and engagement.

Tapping into Trends

It's also hugely valuable for your video strategy to pay attention to trends and to analyse what's happening in and around your industry or area of expertise at any given time throughout the year. You may consider using tools such as Google Trends to find information about searches or keywords that are trending in your industry at different times of the year, or topics that are increasing in search volume over time to become more valuable.

When it comes to understanding trends that are valuable to your audience (and therefore your video strategy) you also can't ignore the 'low hanging fruit' that's often sitting right in front of you in your social media feed, forums or community groups around your area of interest.

By being strategic and paying attention to common questions, topics, conversations or viral content that are surfacing in digital communities around your area of expertise and having somewhere to store these ideas when they surface you'll be able to gather valuable audience insight to feed into your video strategy down the track.

For this purpose, often just having a Google Sheet or central document in which ideas or common questions are noted whenever you or your team come across them is a great place to start.

3. Empathy Mapping

The final customer research strategy I want to share with you is a very powerful exercise that we use with our clients in order to help gain a deeper understanding of what is really going through their audience's heads. This process is called empathy mapping, and the activity uses a simple framework to help brainstorm and develop deeper empathy for your audience.

An empathy map is typically divided into four quadrants representing:

- What they Think
- What they Feel
- What they Say
- What they Do.

THINK	FEEL
SAY	DO

Let's look at each area:

- **Think**—This covers the beliefs, perspectives and questions of your target audience. What problems or pain points are top of mind? How do they think about your industry, your product category or the service provided? What misunderstandings exist?

- **Feel**—This covers the emotions and fears experienced by your audience related to the problem that you solve. What desires drive them? What motivates their interest? What anxieties hold them back? What do they aspire to?

- **Say**—This covers what your audience vocalises publicly about your offerings or industry. What do their conversations reveal about their values and needs? What objections do they raise?

- **Do**—This covers your audience's actions and behaviours. How do they currently solve their problems? What is their purchasing process? What alternatives do they spend time and money on?

Populating each quadrant of an empathy map opens a window into who your audience really is. **It moves you from assumptions to actionable insights.**

- -

Using empathy mapping with a target audience

Here are some key steps for using empathy mapping with a target audience:

1. Define your core audience segment

Avoid falling into the trap of trying to appeal to 'everyone'. Empathy mapping works best when focused on a tightly defined viewer avatar. Get clear on the specific pain points and characteristics of your ideal customer. Use the customer avatars you created earlier in this chapter as your lens through which to build your empathy map.

2. Engage in immersive research

Gather insights through surveys, interviews and social listening. Search reviews and join discussions to observe them candidly. The goal is to collect rich qualitative data, not just demographics. Really dig into their inner world.

NOTE: This step can be skipped if you, or your client already feels that they know their customer avatar well enough. However, beware of making false assumptions that aren't backed by qualitative research.

3. Brainstorm map quadrants

Bring team members or stakeholders together in a room with a large visual empathy map on the wall or whiteboard. Start populating the Think, Feel, Say and Do quadrants with sticky notes generated from your research learnings, experiences and assumptions. Consider using different coloured sticky notes for each section.

4. Uncover connections and gaps

Step back and analyse the map for patterns, contradictions and gaps. Do certain feelings relate to specific thoughts or actions? Are there gaps where you need more data? Let themes and narratives emerge organically from the map.

5. Convert into actionable insights

Synthesise learnings into strategic opportunities. What video content types would address specific pain points? What emotions should your future video strategy appeal to first? Empathy mapping provides a clear picture of how to reach your audience, both with messaging that cuts through, and how, where and in what way you share content online.

Example empathy map

Here is an example empathy map created for a financial services company targeting young professionals:

THINK	FEEL
How can I pay off student loans faster? Does buying a house make sense? What does 'retirement' even mean now? Too anxious and overwhelmed to even start.	Overwhelmed by debt. Dream of financial freedom. Fearful of the future. Skeptical of financial institutions.
SAY	**DO**
'Budgeting feels impossible'. 'Retirement is hopeless for our generation'. 'Banks don't actually care about helping people'.	Avoid looking at bank statements. Spend instead of save Turn to family/friends for financial advice. Research options but take little action.

For this audience, the empathy map reveals anxiety and uncertainty around financial decisions. But it also uncovers their deep desire for clarity and confidence.

This guides the Video Strategist to craft content that first builds trust through transparency and simplicity. Storytelling around achievable goal setting could reduce the overwhelm factor. Sharing perspectives from relatable experts might inspire action.

Brands that don't do the work of empathy mapping can easily miss the mark by only talking about products or complex features. The insights that empathy mapping can uncover reveal genuine human context that strategic video content can be shaped around.

In your role as a Video Strategist, it's important to tap into empathy early and often. Instead of making assumptions, let real data about your viewer's values and motivations guide the way. Creating an empathy map collaboratively taps into the knowledge across your team while exposing gaps.

The foundations are laid

Now that we've developed greater understanding of our target audience; who they are, how they think, why they act, and how we can best resonate our marketing with them; the foundations are now laid for an effective video marketing strategy. This chapter is one of the most detailed in this book for a very good reason. If you fail to take the time to truly understand who your target audience is for your video strategy, you may miss the mark before you even create a single piece of content.

And now, armed with that clarity, we can move to the next element of an effective video strategy and get clear on what we want that audience to actually do for our business.

BONUS MATERIAL

For downloadable worksheets and resources,
head to *engagevideomarketing.com/more*

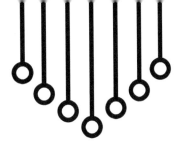

CHAPTER 8

Goals

Imagine getting into your car without any specific destination in mind. You just start driving around randomly, making spur-of-the-moment turns without knowing where you want to ultimately end up. It's unlikely you'll arrive somewhere useful, and you'll definitely waste a lot of fuel on the way.

Similarly, creating videos without concrete goals is like driving around in circles. You're burning time and resources without getting anywhere meaningful.

Having intentional goals provides necessary direction, just like mapping out a destination before a trip. Goals focus your efforts and optimise outcomes. They keep you from getting lost.

Yet many businesses launch into video production without first identifying clear objectives. The result is scattered content without purpose—lots of wasted motion in service of nothing.

Having concrete goals is the second critical element for online video strategy success.

Without clearly defined goals, you end up with videos that have no real impact on your business. You might get some vanity metrics like views or comments, but the content fails to connect with and motivate your audience to action in any meaningful way.

Setting intentional goals eliminates this disconnect. When you identify exactly what you're aiming to achieve upfront, you can then design video content to specifically drive those results. Your content, distribution and optimisation decisions become focused on tangible objectives rather than guesswork.

Developing clarity on your goals requires direct collaboration with the client, or leadership of the business. It is critical at this stage, that as a Video Strategist, you are not working in a bubble. Goals must be defined in close alignment with the objectives of the business in mind.

Conducting a marketing needs analysis

Establishing clear goals is the foundation of an effective video strategy. You should never make assumptions about what a business needs; instead, dig deeper to understand specific objectives and challenges.

Quality questions are the key to uncovering the true needs of a business. To guide this process, you can use a structured framework of questions designed to explore different aspects of the customer journey like we looked at in Chapter 7 with your client or for your business.

Customer Journey Stage	Questions to ask
Awareness	Q1. When you consider the total audience that potentially could be your customer, how many of them are aware that your business actually exists? Q2. Of those that are aware that your business exists, how would you rate their level of understanding of exactly what you do and why you are different from your competitors?
Consideration	Q3. How engaged do you feel that your target market is with your business? Do they regularly see you, hear from you, or somehow get value from you in some form? Q4. How trustworthy and likable do you think your business is to your target audience—not your customers, but those in your market who haven't yet bought from you?
Purchase	Q5. How would you rate your target market's level of desire to actually buy from you? Q6. How effective is your current sales process in converting prospects or leads into clients?
Advocacy	Q7. When you consider your current or past customers, how likely are they to buy from you again? Q8. How valuable are your current and past customers when it comes to driving new business for you, referring other people or spreading the word about your business?

The above line of questioning is designed to unravel assumptions and build a picture of clarity around the business's current effectiveness at attracting, engaging, converting and retaining customers. Consider giving a score out of 10 for each question and using this to rank the business across the four stages to identify potential gaps in the current marketing.

Defining goals for video in a marketing strategy

After going through the process of investigation above, you'll have identified potential gaps in that business's marketing and sales approach that could be filled with strategic video content. Now you can turn your attention to defining the specific goals for any video content you create for that business.

There are different goals that align to each stage of the customer journey and these goals are:

Customer journey stage	Goal
Awareness	Brand positioning
Consideration	Social engagement
Purchase	Conversion
Advocacy	Delight

An effective online video strategy should plan for content that addresses all four goals. However, the priority goals should be based on the gaps you previously identified during the marketing needs analysis process. For the most immediate impact when implementing a video strategy, start where the need is highest, and move forward from there.

UNDERSTAND YOUR CUSTOMER JOURNEY

By linking your video strategy to the customer journey and aligning it with the four main goals—brand positioning, social engagement, conversion, and delight—you can effectively guide your audience from initial awareness to becoming loyal advocates for your brand. Each stage of the journey requires a tailored approach, and understanding these stages allows you to create content that resonates with your audience and drives meaningful results.

The needs and sentiment of the buyer at either end of the customer journey are very different and as such different pieces of video content will engage them as they move through their own journey to 'hopefully' buy what it is you're selling.

Different goals, different content, different ways to use the content online for results.

Let's now break down each of these goals a little further before moving in to Chapter 9, where we'll deep dive into each and introduce you to the different content strategies that work for each particular goal.

Goal 1: Brand positioning

Brand positioning is the crucial first goal in a comprehensive video strategy. At this stage, the focus is on reaching a wide audience who may not yet be familiar with your brand. These individuals, often referred to as a 'cold' audience, are just beginning to recognise a need or feel a 'pain' that could lead them to seek a solution. However, they haven't encountered your business yet.

The primary goal of brand positioning is to turn this cold audience into a warm audience by capturing their attention and making a memorable impression.

To achieve this it's essential to create an emotional connection with your audience. Emotional connections are powerful because they make your brand more relatable and memorable. When people feel an emotional bond with a brand, they are more likely to remember it and consider it when they need a solution to their problem.

Creating this emotional connection requires a deep understanding of your audience's needs, values and aspirations. It involves communicating in a way that speaks directly to these elements, making your brand not just a solution provider but a trusted partner in your audience's journey.

By effectively positioning your brand, you ensure that when potential customers have a need or problem your business can solve, you are one of the first that comes to mind. This is achieved by consistently conveying your brand's values, mission, and unique selling propositions in a way that resonates with your target audience.

Brand positioning is also about establishing trust and building credibility. This groundwork allows the audience to consider your brand seriously in the later stages of their decision-making process.

Effective brand positioning has long-term benefits. It not only increases the likelihood of converting cold audiences into warm leads but also enhances overall brand equity. A well-positioned brand enjoys better recognition, customer loyalty and a stronger market presence. Over time, this can lead to sustained business growth and a competitive edge in the market.

Goal 2: Social engagement

The second goal of social engagement is about building on the relationship and engaging the prospect further as we move them towards the sale.

Back in 2010, author and speaker Bob Burg said:

> *All things being equal, people will do business with*
> *and refer business to those people they know, like*
> *and trust.*

He called this the 'Golden Rule of Networking' and it is this principle that drives an effective social engagement strategy in digital marketing.

In a business, this goal is critical to establish credibility in your market, to show up in the right places, with the right content in the right way. You've begun building a relationship with an audience here, and now you want to deepen that relationship so that you stay top of mind and positively positioned so that when they're ready to buy, they only want to buy from you.

I refer to this goal as social *engagement* quite deliberately, as social *media* is a major factor in *distributing* this style of content, but social media is a tool, not a goal. Making social connections through your video strategy brings an audience alongside you and primes them to be ready to buy from you.

In short, if your business objective is to get more, qualified prospects passed down the funnel ready to buy, then social engagement is where it's at.

Goal 3: Conversion

For this goal, the aim is simple—it's all about making a conversion. Conversion does not necessarily refer to an actual purchase of a product or service (although that is often the case). The outcome might be joining a mailing list, scheduling a sales call, subscribing on social media, whatever the conversion action is for the business, the goal here is to help your ideal client to overcome any objections to taking that action.

At this stage the prospect is basically ready to buy, so if your video strategy fails in delivering on this goal then the prospect will probably buy from someone else, or not buy at all.

For a business, a focus on this goal will become apparent when the aim is to: increase conversion rates, lower the acquisition cost, reduce sales drop-off or lower the time spent selling.

Goal 4: Delight

The fourth goal, delight, focuses on ensuring customer satisfaction and fostering loyalty.

We want our strategic use of video to improve the customer experience, and strengthen the relationships we have with our customers. By using video for the purpose of delighting the clients or customers in ways that keep them engaged longer, and delivering a better experience with your brand, you'll be building loyal advocates and ideally raving fans of your brand. These people will buy again, share their experiences with others, and effectively do your marketing for you through word of mouth.

Business goals aligned to delight might include improved customer retention, higher lifetime value, increased referrals or recurring purchases.

Video is incredibly effective in various formats at achieving each of the four goals however, based on the insight you've now gained on your actual business needs along with an understanding of the business's marketing goals—a video strategy may focus more heavily on creating content for one or two goals rather than an even spread across all four.

These four video strategy goals; together form the backbone of a complete online video strategy that spans the full marketing funnel and aligns with the customer journey and how we think, feel and act as humans—in fact, what we're beginning to understand here, I call the **Full Funnel Video Strategy Framework™** and we're going to dive deeper into the framework as we move into the next chapter and the content element.

BONUS MATERIAL

For downloadable worksheets and resources, head to *engagevideomarketing.com/more*

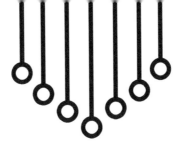

CHAPTER 9

Content

In the previous chapters we established the importance of understanding your audience and then identifying and defining clear goals for your video strategy. We then mapped those goals to the customer journey.

The next important element to understand is content and how an effective video strategy requires a spread of content across the full marketing funnel.

A quick content marketing primer

The term content marketing refers to a strategic marketing approach focused on creating and distributing valuable, relevant and consistent content to attract and engage a clearly defined audience, ultimately driving profitable customer actions.

Unlike traditional advertising, which interrupts consumers with promotional messages, content marketing aims to provide helpful, educational or entertaining content that adds value to the audience's lives.

The roots of content marketing can be traced back to the early 20th century, long before the digital age. One of the earliest examples is the John Deere magazine, *The Furrow*, which was first published in 1895. *The Furrow* provided farmers with valuable information on agricultural techniques and innovations, while also subtly promoting John Deere's products in the process. This publication is considered one of the earliest forms of content marketing because it focused on delivering value to the reader rather than direct advertising.

Another notable example from the early days of content marketing is the soap opera. In the 1930s and 1940s, companies like Procter & Gamble sponsored radio dramas that were designed to appeal to their target audience—housewives. These soap operas provided entertainment while promoting the sponsor's products, hence the name 'soap opera'. This strategy effectively engaged listeners and built brand loyalty by associating the brand with enjoyable content.

With the rise of the internet, content marketing has evolved and expanded significantly. The web is fundamentally built on content. Websites, blogs, social media platforms and forums are all content-driven, providing users with vast amounts of information and entertainment at their fingertips. This digital landscape has created endless opportunities for brands to engage with their audiences through content.

Content marketing on the internet started gaining traction in the early 2000s with the rise of blogging and SEO. Companies realised that by creating valuable content that addressed the needs and interests of their target audience, they could attract organic traffic to their websites. This content-driven approach not only improved search engine rankings but also established the brands as thought leaders in their respective industries.

The power of video for content marketing

Today, video has become a critical component of content marketing. As internet speeds have increased and video production has become more accessible, consumers have shown a strong preference for video content. Video is engaging, easy to consume, and can convey complex information in a concise and entertaining manner.

Video content of this type is incredibly powerful in the middle of the funnel, where potential customers are seeking information and evaluating their options. For instance, explainer videos, product demonstrations and 'how-to' content are all powerful tools for educating and persuading prospects. These videos provide valuable insights and build trust, helping potential customers feel more confident in their decision-making process.

In addition to this, video content can be easily shared across multiple platforms, including social media, websites and email newsletters, amplifying its reach and impact. The interactive nature of video also allows for more dynamic engagement, encouraging viewers to comment, share and take action.

Ultimately, content designed for the goal of social engagement should be considered as 'helpful content', that serves to add value for an audience and move them closer towards buying from the brand or business. This may be content such as how-to videos, FAQs, thought leadership, expert training, educational series, entertainment, edutainment, humorous content or more.

When planning content for an online video strategy, it's crucial to remember that your strategy should inform the content produced, rather than simply emulating what other businesses have done or brainstorming random video ideas.

This is where the Full Funnel Video Strategy Framework™ makes life easier.

FULL FUNNEL VIDEO STRATEGY™ FRAMEWORK

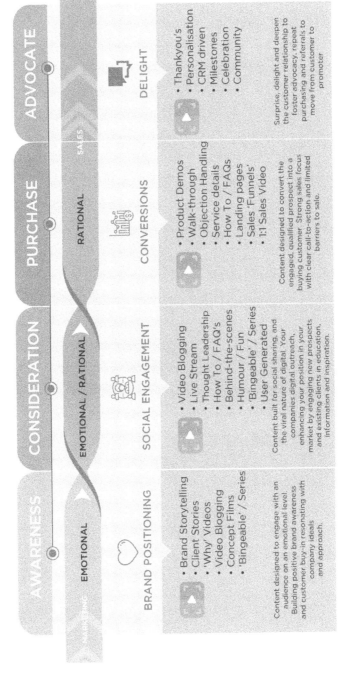

AWARENESS	CONSIDERATION	PURCHASE	ADVOCATE
EMOTIONAL	EMOTIONAL / RATIONAL	RATIONAL	
MARKETING		SALES	
BRAND POSITIONING	SOCIAL ENGAGEMENT	CONVERSIONS	DELIGHT
• Brand Storytelling • Client Stories • 'Why' Videos • Video Blogging • Concept Films • 'Bingeable' / Series	• Video Blogging • Live Stream • Thought Leadership • How To / FAQ's • Behind-the-scenes • Humour / Fun • 'Bingeable' / Series • User Generated	• Product Demos • Walk-through • Objection Handling • Service details • How To / FAQs • Landing pages • Sales 'Funnels' • 1:1 Sales Video	• Thankyou's • Personalisation • CRM driven • Milestones • Celebration • Community
Content designed to engage with an audience on an emotional level. Building positive brand awareness and customer buy-in resonating with company ideals and approach.	Content built for social sharing, and the viral nature of digital. Your companies digital outreach, enhancing your position in your market by engaging new prospects and existing clients in education, information and inspiration.	Content designed to convert the engaged, qualified prospect into a buying customer. Strong sales focus with clear call-to-action and limited barriers to sale.	Surprise, delight and deepen the customer relationship to foster advocacy, repeat purchasing and referrals to move from customer to promoter

The Full Funnel Video Strategy Framework™

When we consider the Full Funnel Video Strategy Framework™ we can quickly understand that the type of videos that work at each stage of the funnel vary considerably as we move from left to right. We're moving from making a strong heart-centred, emotional connection with an audience, through to a rationally induced conversion and then with an intention to provide moments of customer delight. Very different pieces of content need to be considered at each of the stages of the funnel.

For the **top-of-funnel goal of brand positioning**, our content should be grounded in storytelling, an intrinsically human centred form of communication that encourages emotional 'buy in'. This is where we might consider brand stories, client stories, branded content, video blogs or high concept videos that are designed to make an audience sit up, pay attention, and emotionally connect with the brand.

For the **middle-of-funnel social engagement** we need to provide helpful content—videos that further develop the relationship with the audience and position our brand as the right fit for their needs through providing small wins. This is where we'd be looking at creating reels and shorts, video blogs, live videos, how tos or frequently asked questions, event videos, and injecting a bit of personal fun and humour.

Content for the **bottom-of-funnel conversion** needs to address the rational concerns that a prospect has—what questions remain and what do they need to know in order to buy from you. Content created here will directly ask for the sale, and should have limited barriers to an audience taking that action. Conversion content may be product demos or walkthroughs, landing page or sales letter videos, service details videos, sales funnel videos or even one-to-one personalised sales videos.

Then when we move into the **post-conversion delight goal**, content needs to be (or at least feel) very personal and one-on-one. No one gets delighted or feels special when they're sent a piece of advertising. The content here should be personalised, human and used in a natural, authentic way—things like thank you videos, one-to-one video messaging, celebrating customer milestones with a personalised video, or behind-the-scenes type videos letting the customer get to know you and the team better.

Platform Native Content

Before I dive deeper into the types of content for each of the goals outlined above, I need to touch on the fact that certain types of content work better on certain platforms. The distribution channel you use for your video will have an impact on the content's style, language, format and duration (among other things).

The term often used here is 'platform native content'—that is, the content is designed and produced in a way that takes into account the intricacies and audience expectations of the primary platform it will be used on.

Take the example of a video where the goal is social engagement and the content planned out is a how-to video to share with the audience 'how to bake a cake'. The type of video you produce—its format, length and approach to production—would be quite different if the primary distribution channel was YouTube over Instagram.

Over the next four sections, I'm going to unpack for you my suggested content structure, ideas and approach for each of the four goals. Mastering these differences as a Video Strategist will ensure you are well equipped to deliver:

- The right content type
- For the right purpose
- Aligned to the right audience
- At the right time.

Brand Positioning Content

Brand positioning content is pivotal in the marketing funnel, sitting right at the top. Its primary purpose is to engage a previously cold audience—individuals who have never heard of or interacted with your brand. The goal is to capture their attention, establish an emotional connection, and set them on a path that eventually leads to purchasing from you.

At this early stage of the customer journey, the audience is primarily focused on one question: 'What's in it for me?' They are aware of their pain points or problems but are not yet thinking about specific solutions or providers. This stage is all about emotions. The audience is feeling the discomfort or inconvenience of their problem but hasn't yet started thinking about who or what can help them solve it.

To effectively position your brand, the content needs to connect with the audience through the right emotional triggers. This is where the power of storytelling shines in your video strategy. Storytelling in video content allows you to engage your audience emotionally and make your brand memorable.

Video content that takes a storytelling approach should position the customer as the hero of the story, with the brand or business acting as the guide. For your ideal audience to resonate and connect emotionally with the story, they need to see themselves in it. They need to feel that this story is for them, about them, and connects with their experiences and challenges.

When the brand positions itself as the hero, the customer disconnects because their primary concern at this stage is their own needs and pain points. They are not interested in your brand's achievements or history. They are focused on how you can help them, and the content should reflect that perspective[1].

Brand positioning video content should:

1. **Position the customer as the hero:** The narrative would revolve around the customer's journey,

---

[1] I highly recommend reading 'Building a StoryBrand' By Donald Miller to go much deeper into this idea of brand storytelling.

challenges and transformation. Your brand's role is to guide them towards overcoming their issues. This helps in creating a relatable and compelling story that draws the audience in.

2. **Create a relatable and human connection:** The audience needs to see real people and real emotions that they can relate to. This could be through customer interviews, founders' stories, or stories that reflect common challenges and triumphs your audience faces.

3. **Highlight the stakes:** This element makes the audience care about the story and stay engaged. It creates a sense of urgency and importance that keeps the viewer's attention.

4. **Deliver a soft call to action:** The goal of brand positioning content is not to sell but to engage. Therefore, any call to action should be soft and inviting, rather than a hard sales pitch. Think of it as an invitation to learn more about the brand, visit a website, follow on social media or subscribe to a newsletter. This approach nurtures the relationship without overwhelming the audience.

At the brand positioning stage, the focus for your content should be on the emotional outcomes for the audience rather than rational facts and figures about the product. This means creating content that speaks to the audience's emotions, aspirations and values.

People buy from people they feel understand them. Therefore, your brand positioning content should convey that you 'get' them—that you understand their struggles, needs and desires. This is not about selling a product directly but about selling the idea that your brand understands and empathises with the audience.

The ultimate goal of brand positioning content is to encourage the audience to take the next step with your brand. This means moving from passive awareness to active engagement. By creating emotionally compelling content that speaks directly to their needs, you can guide them from being a cold audience to becoming interested and engaged prospects.

The 7 Stages of Brand Storytelling

There is a base structure we use when it comes to brand storytelling videos, and this structure can be easily adapted or refined to suit a range of video approaches, topics and styles and it should be great to get you started. This story structure has been adapted from both Joseph Campbell's *The Hero's Journey* and Donald Miller's *StoryBrand* Framework. I highly recommend further reading from both of these authors.

1. Emotive HOOK

2. Establish PAIN

3. Set up DESIRE

4. Introduce the GUIDE (brand)

5. Show TRANSFORMATION journey

6. Highlight the RESULT (new normal)

7. Call to ACTION

We begin with the **emotive hook**—it's critical across all video content types and distribution channels that this emotive hook grabs your audience in the opening few seconds. If they're a cold audience, and they're only thinking about what's in it for them, then you need to hook them in fast (approximately 1.5—3 seconds depending on the platform)—or the engagement window has past and you've lost the audience.

We then want to establish or **highlight the pain** that the audience is feeling, an emotion that they can relate to and that makes this content instantly relevant to them and their life at this moment. By establishing the pain we've introduced what's at stake and we're preparing the audience to connect with the next stage of the story when we set up the desire.

The **desire sets the story in motion** and should communicate where the story needs to go. We need to set up the positive outcomes that can be reached when working with the brand or product, and allow the audience to really connect with that, and want the same outcome for themselves in their life.

Next we need to **introduce the guide**, which as I explained earlier is the brand, the product or the business that this content is being created for. By introducing the brand in a way that sets it up as a supporter, or tool or vehicle to help the hero win—the audience connects themselves emotionally to the brand and feels that perhaps this brand can help them win too.

We then try to **show the transformation journey**, that is, communicate how the transformation takes place, the ways in which the brand guides the hero, works with them and leads them to success.

And then **highlight the result**—a story needs a conclusion and in a brand's story we need to clearly understand the win that is provided to a customer or client when they engage with the brand. In storytelling terms often the hero character ends the story by returning back to their normal life but it's a new normal—they're a changed person due to the transformation that the brand or product has enabled for them.

And finally, the **soft call to action**. Remember, brand positioning content should not push a hard pitch ... if the content is done well, then the audience has engaged, bought in and is open to accept your invitation to connect further. In certain videos this call to action might be quite explicit such as 'Follow us on Facebook to learn more' or more subtly communicated through the closing lines of dialogue that spurs an audience to action with an emotional pull.

This storytelling structure can be applied, refined, adapted and used across a number of content types from interview-driven, documentary style edits through to animated explainer videos and even video webinars.

Social Engagement Content

Social engagement content could otherwise be thought of as mid-funnel content—videos that are designed to engage with an audience who have started the journey towards solving their need.

At this stage of the customer journey a prospect is actively seeking to engage (or are open to the idea of engaging) with brands or businesses that could potentially solve their problem. As such, the key goal here is to aim to provide education, information, inspiration and (yep!) entertainment to this prospect, to allow them to achieve some small wins towards their desired outcome, and to feel better informed about their options for solving their problem.

Remember, for this goal, we're not about selling—it's about giving value, building relationships and establishing trust. Selling comes later.

For the social engagement goal, two elements need consideration.

The first aspect is 'social'. That means content for this goal needs to be created with human interaction in mind. It's about opening a conversation with your audience and connecting on a human level. (We can also recognise here that it's this goal where your content best integrates with social media. All social media channels are designed to be people to people connection platforms first and foremost, so if social engagement content is created with this in mind, then it'll be more likely to engage the right audiences in the right way to achieve this goal.

The second aspect is 'engagement'. What this really comes down to is how the content you produce will encourage your ideal audience to engage with it through comments, likes, hearts, shares and re-tweets.

Not only is 'engagement' a valuable measure of the success of a video on social media it's also critical in building connections and relationships with an audience in order to move them towards a sale.

An important concept to consider at the social engagement phase is the idea of 'moving the free line' in a business.

Moving the Free Line

In the time before content marketing, traditional marketing centred around direct response tactics. The process was straightforward: See ad → Buy product or See ad → Call us. This approach relied heavily on prompting immediate actions from potential customers. In the digital age, however, engaging consumers online requires a different approach.

The internet is built on a foundation of free offerings. Users expect free email, free websites, free content, free video calls, free instant messaging, free videos and free music. This expectation of free access has fundamentally changed the dynamics of how brands must engage with their audiences online. To capture attention and foster engagement, businesses must be willing to give something of value away for free. This is where the concept of 'moving the free line' comes into play.

The concept of 'moving the free line' is grounded in the principle of demonstrating value before asking for a commitment. In essence, it means providing value without the expectation of immediate compensation. This strategy involves offering free educational content, expertise and knowledge to build trust and establish a relationship with the audience.

In an environment where consumers are often wary of marketing messages and skeptical of brand promises, building trust is paramount. By providing valuable content for free, brands can demonstrate their expertise and reliability. This helps in creating a positive impression and building a strong online reputation. When consumers perceive that a brand is willing to offer genuine value without any immediate strings attached, they are more likely to develop trust and a sense of goodwill towards that brand.

My message to you here is to **lead with value.**

Educational content plays a crucial role in moving the free line. By offering insights, tips, tutorials and how-to guides, brands can position themselves as thought leaders and trusted advisors in their industry. This type of content not only attracts attention but also engages the audience by addressing their pain points and providing solutions. When consumers find the content helpful and relevant, they begin to associate the brand with positive outcomes and expertise.

The Power of Reciprocity

The strategy of moving the free line leverages the psychological principle of reciprocity. When someone receives something of value for free, they feel a natural inclination to reciprocate. In the context of marketing, this means that when consumers benefit from free content, they are more likely to feel positively towards the brand and consider making a purchase in the future. This sense of reciprocity can significantly influence buying decisions and foster brand loyalty.

Moving the free line is not just about immediate engagement;

it also has long-term benefits. By consistently providing value, brands can cultivate a loyal audience base. These loyal customers are not only more likely to make repeat purchases but also become advocates for the brand, spreading positive word-of-mouth and attracting new customers.

This approach also nicely aligns with the buyer's journey we're now so familiar with as Video Strategists. Today's consumers often conduct extensive research in the consideration phase before making a purchase. By offering free educational content, brands can be part of this research process, influencing consumers' perceptions and decisions early on. This positions the brand as a go-to resource, increasing the likelihood of conversion when the consumer is ready to buy.

Remember, the goal for social engagement content is to deepen the relationship with your ideal audience—and to move them closer to the sale. You're not trying to sell to them right now (although that might happen).

As such the call to action for any content in the social engagement phase should be an invitation to engage further, such as:

- Ask a question
- Leave a comment
- Subscribe
- Like
- Share
- Learn more.

In many cases social engagement videos often become the core strategic video type that a brand will implement, as video for this goal—at its heart—is just good, solid **content marketing**. And content marketing, done right and on a consistent basis, will continue to deliver a return on the investment for the long term.

Conversion Content

Conversion content sits squarely at the bottom of the funnel—the pointy end—and the key goal here in most cases is to convert the qualified, engaged prospect into a customer. In other cases the conversion may be a non-financial commitment such as confirming a meeting, joining an email list or attending an event, but in either case the conversion here comes when an audience makes a commitment to move forward with a brand or business.

At this stage of the customer journey a prospect should be primed to buy, although they have not yet made the final decision. Content for this goal should, therefore, be focused on the removal of any blockages that might be preventing someone from converting.

We need to be providing rational information at this stage, answering any specific questions that a prospect has, allowing them to see 'behind the curtain' at what they will get when they make the decision to buy. Although emotion is still at play here, this has now taken a back seat to the rational part of the brain so the video content needs to be able to rationalise what the emotional brain is telling someone.

This is where the sales pitch needs to happen.

As an audience is effectively saying to you, 'Okay, I'm interested, and this looks like something that I need to solve my problem, so … sell it to me.'

And the power of video is very evident here. When done right, conversion focused video content has the ability to humanise the sales process in a way that is otherwise somewhat lost in our online and digital world.

Years ago we lived in what you could therefore call a 'low-tech, high-touch' world where basically every business interaction was a direct human to human connection. Today, we live and consume in what could be described as a 'low-touch, high-tech' world—the technologies that surround us have, in many cases, removed the human touch element to business.

If we wanted to buy a TV, we used to walk in to an electronics store and speak with a salesperson who talked us through to a sale. Low-tech, high-touch.

Now, we're much more likely to make that buying decision online, and either transact right there in an online store, or simply walk into the retailer knowing exactly what we want to buy and how much it costs. High-tech, low-touch.

Despite this, we are still people—and people want to buy from people. So where great marketing and sales really stand out today is when the high-touch can be brought back to a high-tech world.

How Zappos leverage video
to boost ecommerce conversions

Zappos, a pioneer in online retail, has harnessed the power of video to drive higher conversion rates on their ecommerce platform. From early on in the company's journey Zappos understood that one of the key barriers for their audience when buying shoes online came from the fact that most people wanted to see the shoes in real life, to try them on and get a feel for whether they would suit them.

In order to somewhat remove this barrier Zappos began to focus on producing short videos to enhance their product descriptions, providing a dynamic and interactive way to showcase their products. For example, Zappos includes videos to demonstrate the flexibility of a boot or the texture of a fabric—details that photos alone might not fully convey. These videos help customers make more informed purchasing decisions by giving them a clearer understanding of the product's features and benefits.

Zappos have also leaned into the fact that videos are a powerful tool for increasing customer engagement. Because video captures and holds attention longer than text and images alone, Zappos discovered that including videos on product pages increased the time customers spend on their site, a key indicator of engagement.

Authenticity is also a core component of Zappos's video strategy. Their product videos are designed to be honest and realistic, avoiding exaggerated or misleading representations. This transparency builds trust with customers, making them more likely to complete a purchase. Zappos often features real people demonstrating products in everyday scenarios, adding to the authenticity and relatability of the content.

They also demonstrate the value of product videos in addressing common customer concerns and questions. By visually demonstrating how a product works or fits, Zappos reduces the uncertainty that can lead to hesitation or cart abandonment. For instance, seeing a shoe's flexibility and comfort in a video can reassure a customer about its quality, which text descriptions might not fully convey.

The impact of video on conversion rates for Zappos is substantial with video contributing to higher conversion rates (up to 30% lift) by enhancing the shopping experience and reducing the likelihood of returns.

Zappos also leverages feedback from video comments and customer reviews to refine their product offerings and video content. This iterative process helps them stay aligned with customer needs and preferences, leading to continuous improvement in their marketing strategies and product designs.

As digital marketing evolves, Zappos adapts to changes in social media algorithms by emphasising engaging, high-quality video content. Recognising that video content often receives higher engagement on platforms like Facebook and Instagram, Zappos focuses on creating visually appealing and informative videos that are tailored to these platforms.

As Zappos has demonstrated, in simple terms, conversion videos ideally can be thought of as replacing the job that a salesperson does in an offline transaction.

The type of video you may be considering here could be:

- Product demonstration videos
- How-tos or FAQs that are specific to your business or product
- Walkthrough videos that show people what they get when they buy
- Sales videos that deliver a pitch or a clear and compelling offer
- An 'objection busting' video that addresses common concerns people have that hold them back from buying
- A 'video sales letter' (VSL) that explains your offer in detail and why people should consider making the purchase.

Importantly, video here does not need to be highly produced, or particularly creative to be effective. It should be direct, clear and answer any questions that a prospect has that moves them directly towards the sale.

The videos should also be relevant to just one product, service or conversion goal. (Which means an effective strategy will see you create different videos for each product or service that you need to sell.)

Critically, the videos should be used in such a way that limits barriers to a sale. If your content does its job of convincing someone that they want to buy, then you need to ensure you make it easy for them to click that buy button and complete the transaction.

Delight Content

When planning your content for the goal of delight, there are many approaches you can take, but the key principle is that the video content should aim to deepen the customer relationship and foster a stronger affinity with your brand. This stage of the customer journey is all about **transforming satisfied customers into enthusiastic advocates** who are eager to share their positive experiences with others.

Delighting customers means exceeding their expectations in ways that make them feel valued and appreciated. Video content at this stage should be human-centred and personalised, reaching out to customers in unexpected and delightful ways. These videos often have a lower production value (think smartphone, selfie-style videos) but pack a significant emotional punch. When a business's systems and staffing allow it, integrating personalised video outreach into customer experience processes can be a highly effective strategy for delight.

Key touchpoints for creating delight

To create impactful delight videos, it's essential to analyse your customer experience across your range of products or services and pinpoint key touchpoints that could be enhanced with video.

- **Addressing buyer's remorse post-purchase:**
  Buyers often experience regret or doubt after
  making a purchase. A personalised video message
  thanking them for their purchase, reassuring them
  of the benefits, and expressing excitement about
  their decision can help mitigate this remorse and
  enhance their overall experience.

- **Onboarding new customers:** When a product or
  service is delivered, a follow-up video can re-engage the
  customer with your brand. This video can include tips
  on getting the most out of their purchase, encouraging
  them to share their experience with others, or inviting
  them to join your community.

- **Reducing churn:** For subscription or recurring
  revenue-based models, identifying typical drop-off
  points is crucial. Personalised video messages can
  reinspire customers who are at risk of unsubscribing
  or ending agreements by highlighting new features,
  offering exclusive benefits, or simply reminding them
  of the value they receive from your service.

- **Celebrating milestones:** If your product or service
  leads to specific, measurable milestones for your
  customer, celebrating these moments with a
  personalised video can significantly enhance their
  experience. Congratulatory messages for anniversaries,
  usage milestones or achievements can make customers
  feel recognised and appreciated.

- **Personalised support responses:** Addressing support
  tickets or help queries through personalised video
  not only develops a stronger human connection but

can also be more effective in resolving issues. A video response can provide a more detailed and nuanced explanation than text alone, helping to build trust and satisfaction.

- **Humanising invoices:** Including a friendly video message from an account manager with every invoice can remind the customer of their value to your business, transforming a routine transaction into an opportunity to deepen the relationship.

Tools and processes to deliver delight

Now we've covered the potential touchpoints, let's look at some practical tools and processes you could adopt to deliver delight for your business through your video strategy.

- **One-to-one videos:** Personalised videos, such as a business owner sending a short LinkedIn message to a long-term client to say thank you, can create a strong impact. These videos show that you genuinely care about your customers as individuals.

- **Automated personal videos:** Using apps like BombBomb, Vidyard or Bonjoro, you can automate the sending of personal videos for actions such as signing up to a mailing list or purchasing a product. These tools allow for automated prompting to create and send a personalised video in a timely manner, ensuring each customer feels special and appreciated (and it becomes part of your organisation's SOPs).

- **Integration with Customer Relationship Management (CRM) systems:** For larger operations, integrating video into your CRM using tools like Vidyard or HubSpot can help scale personalised video messages. Automated workflows can trigger video messages based on customer actions, ensuring timely and relevant communication that enhances the customer experience.

Incorporating video into your strategy for delighting customers requires thoughtful planning and execution. By focusing on personalised, human-centred content that reaches customers at key touchpoints, you can transform satisfied customers into passionate advocates. This stage of the customer journey is crucial for building lasting relationships and driving sustained business growth. As effective Video Strategists, harnessing the power of delight can become one of your secret weapons in achieving a full-funnel video strategy.

Now that we've got our content strategically mapped out based on our audience and goals for our video strategy, it's time to consider how we'll distribute that content and get it in front of the right people.

BONUS MATERIAL

For downloadable worksheets and resources, head to *engagevideomarketing.com/more*

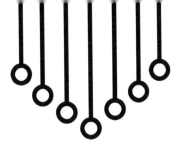

CHAPTER 10

Distribution

This is where the expertise of a confident Video Strategist truly shines in defining an effective video strategy. Distribution is the element that often overwhelms or is mishandled by many businesses approaching video tactically rather than strategically.

It is critical that we take a strategic approach to distribution, making informed decisions about platforms, posting strategies, publication frequency, content amplification, and more, all aligned with what we've learnt and identified when breaking down audience, goals and content.

Distribution is all about using your videos:

- On the right platforms
- In the right way
- To ensure maximum return on video investment.

This chapter:

- Provides an overview of approaching distribution strategically
- Discusses the right mindset to adopt in this ever-changing landscape of video distribution platforms
- Outlines recommended approaches to maximise video distribution effectively.

Before we get into the above, I want to alleviate a fear you probably have: you do not need to be an expert in every single video and social media platform to design and implement an effective video strategy. Platforms will come and go, and best practices on each platform will evolve. Your focus should be on understanding each platform enough to know where it fits within your strategy and, where necessary, to gain deeper knowledge or expert help relevant to specific video strategies.

Currently, your distribution focus will likely be on YouTube, Facebook, Instagram and LinkedIn. However, for some strategies and clients, platforms like TikTok, X (formerly Twitter), Snapchat, Pinterest,or even Twitch may need to be prioritised.

Fish where the fish are

This is the key mindset for effective distribution. It requires you to understand where your audience spends their time online so you can create video content native to those primary platforms. By doing so, your content will be more effective in engaging your audience and driving them to action, especially for top-of-funnel content targeting audiences in the awareness stage.

Deep understanding of your audience, as discussed in earlier sections of this book, is crucial here. For example, if your audience is primarily on Instagram, creating short, visually engaging videos for Instagram Stories or Reels will likely be more effective than longer-form content.

Aligning Distribution with Goals

Aligning the distribution platform with the intended action is vital. Different goals require different approaches:

- **Brand positioning:** If the goal is brand positioning and the intended action is for the audience to learn more on your website, YouTube might be the primary distribution platform. Utilising YouTube end screens or hyperlinks in the description can drive viewers to take the desired action. Alternatively, you may be better off using a Vimeo or Wistia embed on a key page of your website to drive the desired action.

- **Social engagement:** If the goal is social engagement then you're likely going to be focusing your efforts on the social media specific distribution channels such as YouTube, Facebook, Instagram, TikTok or LinkedIn. This will be content designed to capitalise on the social nature of these platforms and encourage people to engage with the content to increase virality.

- **Conversions:** If the goal is conversion, where the intended action is to get a viewer to add a product to their online shopping cart and place an order, an embedded video on the product listing page of your website is more appropriate. Platforms like Wistia, which allow for seamless integration with ecommerce functionality, are ideal for this purpose.

- **Delight:** And if you're distributing for the purposes of delight, then you'll want to consider which platform is best suited to serving this video to the intended audience and leading them more clearly to the action you want them to take. For example, a personalised video recorded on Vidyard and sent via text message might be the ideal way to go.

Which platform is best?

Each video distribution platform has its unique characteristics and best practices. Here is a brief overview of which platforms are typically best for when it comes to delivering on certain goals:

- **YouTube:** The world's second-largest search engine and a crucial platform for video content. It's ideal for brand positioning, educational content and long-form videos. YouTube's SEO capabilities also make it a powerful tool for discoverability, particularly when capitalising on the YouTube Shorts feature alongside longer form content.
- **Facebook:** With its massive user base and sophisticated targeting options, Facebook is excellent for a wide range of video content, from short ads and Facebook Reels

to live videos. Facebook's algorithm favours engaging content that generates interaction, so prioritise videos that encourage likes, shares and comments.

- **Instagram:** Best for visually appealing, short-form content. Instagram Stories, Live and Reels offer various ways to engage with your audience. The platform is particularly effective for lifestyle and short-form brand storytelling content.

- **LinkedIn:** Ideal for B2B content, professional development videos and industry insights. LinkedIn's professional audience is more receptive to informative and educational content that provides value (however is also starting to move more towards short-form TikTok style content as of the time of writing this book).

- **TikTok:** A rapidly growing platform known for its short, engaging and often viral content. TikTok is excellent for reaching audiences of increasingly wider demographics with creative and entertaining videos.

- **Snapchat:** Similar to Instagram in its focus on short, engaging content. It's particularly effective for real-time engagement and behind-the-scenes content.

- **Pinterest:** A visual discovery engine that works well for how-to videos, DIY projects and product demonstrations. It's a great platform for driving traffic to your website.

- **Twitch:** Primarily a live streaming platform popular with gamers but increasingly used by brands for live events, product launches and real-time engagement.

A tiered distribution strategy

With a strategic approach to each video we can be much clearer on which distribution method will be most suitable in order to ensure maximum effectiveness of the video. From there we can select that as our video's primary distribution channel and focus our efforts there.

So, for each video we need to determine first and foremost the primary distribution platform. That is, the video platform that provides the best method of publication for this video in order to ensure the video reaches the right audience in the right way.

Critically, there should be only one primary distribution platform. Decide on the main platform for each video and don't try to make a video that's ideal for multiple platforms.

TIERED DISTRIBUTION STRATEGY

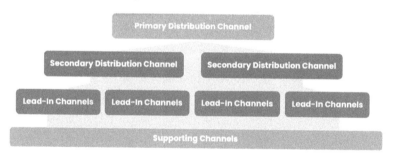

Every social media platform and video distribution method has its own native uniqueness, and although there are often similarities and shared audiences across multiple platforms— it is simply less effective to produce a video that tries to 'fit' multiple platforms.

DISTRIBUTION

Once the primary distribution channel has been determined, we can then decide on a few secondary distribution channels across which the video can be repurposed or reshared. In some cases, you'll be wanting to produce different variations of the primary content to suit a secondary platform. In others the video may just be shared as it is on the primary platform, for increased exposure.

The primary channel can be considered your growth channel—that is, the platform that is a brand's key content focus, where the majority of your audience hangs out or where your content is best suited for maximum engagement and results.

Your strategy for your secondary channels then is to engage with the content whilst also encouraging an audience to move to the primary channel for more.

Then, I also recommend strategising some additional 'lead-in' channels. On these platforms you'll be wanting to create and distribute teaser video content with the goal of driving an audience directly to the primary channel to watch more. A good strategy here is to create short, cut-down versions of the full video produced specifically for each platform with a strong call to action to encourage viewers to watch the full video on the primary platform.

Finally, you'll want to strategise any 'supporting channels' in which you'll be able to make use of other content types such as emails, images, podcasts, Instagram stories or even GIFs that will be able to increase awareness of the primary video, and encourage a viewer to head on over to the primary channel and take a look.

TIERED DISTRIBUTION STRATEGY

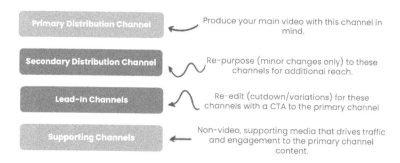

Let's look at an example of this tiered distribution strategy in which YouTube is decided to be the primary distribution channel.

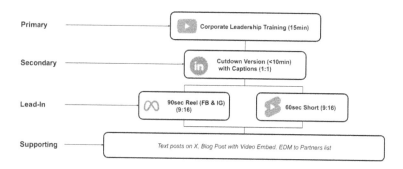

In this case, the brand has determined that YouTube will be their primary growth channel, so the goal as we move down the tiers is to drive as many views as we can to their YouTube video from other channels.

So the primary video is published on YouTube—in this case it's a 15-minute high value training video all about corporate leadership for the goal of social engagement. From this, it's determined that LinkedIn is a highly valuable platform for engaging this target audience so LinkedIn will be the secondary channel. A slight variation is made to the YouTube version of the video cutting it down to under 10 minutes and editing it into a square format with burnt in captions to create a native LinkedIn video. When it's published to LinkedIn the post text mentions the full video over on YouTube and a link to the primary video is included in the first comment.

Next, two further edits are created as lead-in content, a 90-second teaser in vertical ratio and using dynamic captions for Instagram Reels and a 60-second video for YouTube Shorts. Both of these teasers give value in and of themselves but have a strong call to action included encouraging a viewer to watch the full training over on YouTube.

Finally, supporting channels are used with additional traffic driven to the YouTube video through a series of tweets, a blog post is written with the video embedded, and an email campaign is sent out.

There you have it—a strategic and highly effective distribution strategy has been implemented for that video—and it's now set up for success.

Distribution frequency and timing

When implementing a tiered distribution strategy for your videos, it's crucial to make strategic decisions regarding the frequency and timing of publication across various platforms. Both frequency and timing significantly impact the effectiveness of your video strategy.

- **Frequency:** refers to how often video content will be published on each platform. The simple rule here is that there is no one-size-fits-all answer. The optimal frequency depends on several factors, including your audience's preferences, the nature of the platform and the type of content you're producing. For example, platforms like YouTube favour longer, more in-depth content that can be published less frequently, such as once a week or even bi-weekly. In contrast, platforms like Instagram and TikTok thrive on shorter, more frequent posts, often requiring daily or multiple posts per week to maintain engagement.

- **Timing:** refers to the specific time of day and day of the week when it's best to publish your videos. Again, there's no universal answer, as optimal posting times can vary widely depending on your audience demographics and behaviour patterns. The best approach to determine the right timing for your strategy is to analyse the available data. Each platform provides insights and analytics that can help you understand when your audience is most active and engaged. For example, YouTube Analytics offers detailed reports on viewer activity, allowing you to pinpoint the best times to release new content. Similarly, Instagram Insights can show you the peak activity hours of your followers, enabling you to schedule posts for maximum visibility.

My caution here, is to not get too bogged down on this decision. After all, a video is better published than not. So just get it out there, and let it run if you're not sure about when to do it.

Importance of consistency

Regardless of the specific frequency and timing you choose, one of the keys to a successful distribution strategy is consistency. Regularly releasing videos on a consistent schedule—such as the same day and time each week—helps build anticipation and reliability among your audience. When viewers know when to expect new content, they are more likely to engage with it regularly.

Consistency also signals to platform algorithms that your account is active and reliable, which can boost your content's visibility. For example, consistently posting high-quality videos can help your YouTube audience stay more engaged with your content sending positive signals to the algorithm. While regular activity on Instagram can increase your chances of appearing in followers' feeds and explore pages.

Adapting based on data

While consistency is crucial, it's equally important to remain adaptable. Continuously monitor the performance of your videos and be willing to adjust your frequency and timing based on the insights you gather. If data shows that your audience engages more on certain days or times, adjust your schedule accordingly to maximise engagement.

Additional distribution considerations

When strategically planning your video distribution, it's essential to consider how you can leverage both online and offline networks to maximise the reach of your content. By tapping into various networks, you can significantly amplify your video's visibility and engagement, often reaching an exponentially larger audience.

Here are some examples.

Online networks

- **Industry influencers:** Collaborating with industry influencers is a powerful way to expand your reach. Influencers have established credibility and large followings in your niche, which can provide a significant boost to your video's visibility. By having an influencer share or endorse your content, you tap into their audience, gaining access to potential customers who trust their recommendations.

- **LinkedIn newsletters and groups:** LinkedIn is a robust platform for professional networking. Sharing your videos in LinkedIn newsletters and groups related to your industry can drive targeted traffic. Engaging with active discussions and providing valuable content in these groups can position you as a thought leader and attract more viewers to your videos.

- **X (Twitter) Spaces and audio rooms:** Audio-based platforms like X Spaces offer real-time engagement opportunities. Participating in or hosting audio rooms where you discuss relevant topics and share your video content can create immediate interest and drive viewers to your content. It's a dynamic way to interact with your audience and provide value.

- **Blogs and guest posting:** Popular blogs in your niche often have dedicated readerships. Writing guest posts that include your videos or being featured in industry blogs can enhance your video's reach. This method also boosts your SEO and drives organic traffic from established platforms.

- **Facebook groups and trending hashtags:** Facebook groups centred around your industry or interests are excellent for sharing your videos. These groups often have engaged members who are interested in specific topics. Additionally, using trending hashtags on platforms like X and Instagram can increase the discoverability of your content by tapping into ongoing conversations.

Offline networks

- **Referral partners, colleagues and staff:** Leveraging your business's referral partners, colleagues and particularly your staff can extend your video's reach beyond your immediate network. Encouraging them to share your videos with their clients or contacts can introduce your content to new, relevant audiences.

- **Industry publications and printed collateral:** Industry publications, whether online or in print, offer credibility and reach. Featuring your videos in these publications can significantly boost visibility. Additionally, printed collateral in stores or events that include QR codes linking to your videos can drive offline audiences online.

- **QR codes on packaging:** Including QR codes on your product packaging that link to video content is a practical way to engage customers post-purchase. These videos can provide additional information, tutorials, or simply enhance the customer experience, fostering a deeper connection with your brand.

Integrating a strategic approach to tapping into both online and offline networks can exponentially increase the reach and impact of your video content. By leveraging the credibility and established audiences of influencers, engaging in professional networks, participating in real-time audio discussions, contributing to blogs, and utilising referral partnerships and printed materials, you create a multifaceted distribution strategy that maximises visibility and drives meaningful engagement with your target audience.

This is an aspect of video marketing that I constantly see overlooked, and it can be a hidden goldmine for reach and engagement.

What's actually important here?

When it comes to designing an effective distribution strategy for any video, it's important that the approach taken is grounded by the other strategic elements we've discussed. That is, the distribution strategy makes sense for the content planned, works with the goal for the video and aligns directly with the intended audience.

Not every video necessarily needs to go viral and accumulate millions of views in 24 hours. To be effective, some videos only need to be viewed 20 times by the right high-value clients who are ready to take action.

Paid amplification strategy

Any discussion around video distribution online simply can't ignore the importance of paid amplification strategies.

As Video Strategists I believe our role is to build out the video roadmap for a business aligned to specific goals, and then to work alongside our team or our clients to implement the strategy. Depending on your specific skill set and interests you may either bring paid amplification services and specialisation into your team, or when necessary, partner with a third party platform specialist to set up and manage paid campaigns for you or your clients.

I believe that the key mindset to adopt when it comes to paid advertising online is to **focus on organic content strategy first**, and *then* **use paid amplification to increase reach and targeting**.

By going through the frameworks in this book, you'll already be planning for video content that will move your audience to take action. When greater reach, more specific targeting, or retargeting is required to achieve the desired results, this is where paid amplification really becomes important in your overall strategy.

If your content plan is misaligned with your audience, your messaging not connected to the right stage in the customer journey, or your videos are too focused on the brand—it doesn't matter how much you pay for amplification, it won't yield the desired results. Your ad spend will end up being too high to deliver any ROI.

The best way to consider paid campaign strategy in my opinion, is to use paid spend to simply tighten up and accelerate the funnel.

Where an organic video strategy will likely see customers coming in to the funnel at all stages, and moving through the funnel at various speeds, with all sorts of potential twists and turns—a strategically designed **paid** video campaign should allow for a much clearer and more direct journey for a prospect to take through to conversion.

- -

Example of a simple paid video funnel

You start with a cold (but defined!) audience.

Video ad number 1 is served to this audience on the right platform at the right time, and should be a brand positioning ad. This could potentially be a longer form video, perhaps 1-5 minutes in duration, and needs to really engage the audience emotionally, recognising the relevant pain points, and moving them to take action.

Then, through video retargeting, or just by sequential distribution of ads, video ad number 2 is served to the audience, but this time as a social engagement ad—one that provides value, educates or informs. The goal with the social engagement stage of the ad funnel is to build trust and further connection between the audience and your solution. You'll want to identify concerns, and objections, and address those through the messaging shared in these ads.

The call to action for video ad number 2 is to a landing page or sales page. It's on this sales page where video ad number 3 is seen. This is the conversion video ad, and the aim for this video is to pitch and sell the product or service to what is now a warm, engaged audience and make a conversion.

As you can see, a simple video ad funnel, structured as a paid campaign still has the same basic strategy as organic content.

Note: before you hit send and fill my inbox with your feedback on the above, I totally recognise that this is an overly simplified example of paid social strategy. It is important to consider expert guidance and advice when investing in paid campaigns at any real scale.

Depending on the ads platform there are a range of possible ways to implement a video ad funnel such as this, multiple possible retargeting options, and ways to segment your audience which effectively would allow variations of this funnel to be served to different people at different times.

Another important element to consider when implementing strategic paid video campaigns is to get clear on how you will measure the ROI and determine success of the campaign. The metrics for paid campaigns become the single most important thing to analyse in order to optimise an ad funnel. Looking at the available numbers, and determining what this analysis means for your ad funnel you can begin to understand how to tweak, adapt, change and refine your video advertising to improve key metrics, and therefore return higher on the ad spend.

When it comes to your mindset around paid amplification as a Video Strategist I want you to focus on planning for content with the same respect for the audience, and their customer journey as you would for organic (or non-paid) content. Be strategic about the paid platform you are advertising on, and ensure you're working out the desired metrics to pay attention to to analyse the ROI for your ad spend. (More on that coming very soon in Chapter 12.)

A final note on paid video advertising: unless it is going to be your specialty, I absolutely recommend partnering with expert ad buyers, or outsourcing the implementation of your campaigns to performance marketers. These people can ensure the finer points connect and are fully optimised to ensure your video amplification is effective.

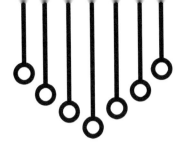

CHAPTER 11

Optimisation

Now that we've laid down solid foundations for an effective video strategy, it's time to focus on the steps we'll take once our videos are published on various distribution platforms to ensure they are set up for success. This brings us to the fifth element of Video Strategy, optimisation.

In this chapter, we will delve into some of the technical aspects of video optimisation, but the primary focus will be on understanding the considerations and approach to take when thinking about optimisation—regardless of platform.

Before we do that, however, it's crucial to grasp the overarching mindset and concepts behind strategically optimising your videos.

What is video optimisation?

Video optimisation involves taking steps to ensure your videos are seen by the right audience in the right way on your chosen platforms. Without proper optimisation, even the most perfectly crafted video content, aligned with your business goals and tailored to your audience, will struggle to reach the majority of your target market.

Imagine you have a comprehensive distribution strategy in place: your primary channel is determined, secondary channels are locked and loaded, and lead-in channels are set up to drive traffic back. Despite this, without optimisation, your videos may still not be seen by your target audience. This is what we aim to influence through optimisation.

To really begin to master video optimisation, we need to understand the mechanisms that determine what content is seen online. That is—the *filters* that lie between us as consumers of online content and the platforms that distribute the content to our eyeballs.

I believe that this process can be broken down into two types of filters:

- **Platform filters:** refer to the algorithms used by distribution platforms to determine which content is displayed to users. These algorithms act as gatekeepers, deciding what content makes it to the viewer's feed and what doesn't. The concept is similar to SEO where the Google algorithm dictates search result rankings. For video content, platforms like YouTube, Facebook and Instagram have their own algorithms that filter and prioritise content based on various factors.

- **Human filters:** involve the viewer's personal decision-making process. Even if a video passes through the platform's algorithmic filter, it must still capture the viewer's attention. This means the content must be compelling enough to make a person stop scrolling, click play and engage with it. If a video fails to engage viewers, it won't achieve its desired impact, regardless of its visibility.

The two main types of optimisation

The role of optimisation in your video strategy is to ensure your content navigates through both the platform and human filters effectively. By understanding these layers and how they apply to each platform and audience, you can implement specific tactics to enhance your content's visibility and engagement.

Based on the filtering systems we've identified above, we can categorise optimisation into two main types:

- Audience optimisation
- Algorithm optimisation.

Let's break it down.

Audience optimisation

This first aspect to optimisation is what I believe is the most important to get right. I call this audience optimisation and it's based on the human layer of the filter system I mentioned above.

In order to reach a particular person with a particular video, you need to break through their personal attention filters. Not only do they need to see the video as they scroll through the content on a social media platform, they also need to engage with the video—watch or click play.

So there are three things we need to consider when it comes to audience optimisation:

- Attention
- Retention
- Action

Attention: Capturing the right eyeballs

The first step in audience optimisation is grabbing the attention of your ideal viewers. Without attention, the rest of your video doesn't matter. When it comes to capturing attention, it's the first few seconds of your video that are crucial. These initial moments, often referred to as the 'hook', determine whether a viewer will continue watching or scroll past. With the average human attention span dwindling and the sheer volume of content available online, capturing and holding a viewer's attention quickly has never been more important.

The concept of the hook in video marketing is like the opening sentence of a novel or the first scene of a movie. It sets the stage, grabs attention, and entices the audience to continue engaging with the content. According to a study by Microsoft, the average human attention span has decreased from 12 seconds in the year 2000 to about 8 seconds today. This means marketers have a very narrow window to make an impact and prevent viewers from moving on to the next piece of content.

Cognitive psychology provides insights into why the first few seconds are so vital. Humans are naturally drawn to interesting and unexpected stimuli. When our brains encounter something new or surprising, it triggers a response that shifts our focus and curiosity. This is why incorporating unexpected elements, vivid imagery or intriguing sounds in the opening seconds can be highly effective in capturing attention.

A report by Facebook IQ found that 65% of people who watch the first three seconds of a video will watch for at least 10 seconds, and 45% will watch for 30 seconds. This data underscores the importance of those initial moments in retaining viewership and suggests that if you can capture attention quickly, there is a higher chance that viewers will stay engaged for a longer duration.

Techniques for an effective hook

Creating an effective hook involves several techniques that leverage visual, auditory and textual elements to grab attention.

- **Visuals:** High-impact visuals are a powerful tool for capturing attention. This can include vibrant colours, dynamic movements or unusual camera angles. Human faces, especially those showing strong emotions, can also draw viewers in. A close-up shot of a person expressing surprise or excitement, for instance, can be highly engaging. Unusual or exciting locations can pique interest. For example, starting a video with someone standing on the edge of a cliff can be a compelling visual hook. Or consider unexpected camera angles or movement to capture attention. Whether it's a high angle looking down or a low angle looking up, or a handheld camera moving alongside the action, the unexpected can be very engaging.

- **Audio:** Sound plays a critical role in capturing attention. The right audio elements can serve as a 'dog whistle' for your target audience, capturing their interest instantly. This can include a startling sound effect, a catchy piece of music, or the opening words spoken in a compelling manner. According to the research by Wistia, videos with engaging audio elements tend to have higher viewer retention rates.

- **Text:** Textual elements, such as bold headlines or dynamic captions, can also be effective. These can be overlaid on the video to provide context or highlight key messages. For example, a bold, intriguing statement like *Discover the secret to doubling your sales* can pique curiosity and encourage viewers to keep watching.

- **The promise:** A clear and compelling promise can hook viewers by setting expectations about what they will gain from watching the video. This promise should be communicated within the first few seconds through the title, thumbnail or opening lines. For instance, a video titled *How to* *lose 10 pounds in one month* immediately tells the viewer what benefit they can expect, which can be a strong motivator to continue watching.

Understanding how the algorithms on different platforms prioritise content is also crucial. Platforms like YouTube and Facebook reward videos that can capture and retain attention quickly. These algorithms often boost content that demonstrates high engagement in the first few seconds, as it indicates that the content is likely to be relevant and engaging for a broader audience.

There is no doubt that the best content creators and marketers have mastered the art of the hook. For example, MrBeast, often starts his videos with outrageous statements or visual stunts that immediately grab attention. His video, *I Spent 50 Hours in Solitary Confinement,* begins with a high-energy introduction directly delivering on the outlandish promise quickly sets the stage for an engaging narrative.

Similarly, brands like Dollar Shave Club have used strong hooks in their viral videos. Their famous ad starts with the CEO delivering a humorous and bold statement, immediately grabbing the viewer's attention and setting the tone for the rest of the video.

On the other hand, failing to recognise the importance of the first few seconds can lead to significant losses in viewer engagement. A study by HubSpot found that 33% of viewers will stop watching a video after 30 seconds, 45% by one minute, and 60% by two minutes. Videos that fail to capture attention quickly are at a higher risk of being abandoned early, leading to lower engagement rates and diminished returns on investment.

Retention: Keeping your audience engaged

Once you've successfully captured your audience's attention with a compelling hook, the next crucial step is to keep them engaged throughout your video. Video retention is about maintaining **relevance** and **interest**, ensuring that viewers stay with your content from start to finish.

The foundation of video retention lies in the **general relevance** of your content to your audience. Understanding your audience's pain points, aspirations and what they find entertaining or valuable is what's important here. Tailoring your content to meet these interests is the key to maintaining their engagement.

There's also **contextual relevance** to consider. The context in which your audience is watching your video plays a significant role in retention. For instance, a video tutorial on how to change a tyre should be concise and practical, addressing the immediate needs of someone likely watching it in a time of urgency. Conversely, a detailed review of the best tyres for off-roading can afford to be longer and more comprehensive, catering to an audience in a research phase. Understanding this context allows you to tailor your content appropriately, thereby enhancing retention.

You'll also want to consider **platform relevance**. The fact is that different video distribution platforms have unique engagement norms and expectations. Adapting your content to fit these norms can significantly impact video retention.

- On **YouTube** (for example), using tactics like pattern interrupts, cut scenes and engaging transitions can help keep viewers watching longer. Pattern interrupts are sudden changes in the flow of the video that re-engage the viewer's attention, such as switching from a talking head to an illustrative animation. These techniques break the monotony and refresh the viewer's interest.

- On platforms like **TikTok** and **Instagram Reels**, leveraging trending formats, quick cuts and interactive elements like polls or questions can maintain engagement. These platforms thrive on short, dynamic content that captures attention quickly and keeps it through continuous engagement tactics.

And finally, you'll want to consider **funnel stage relevance**. That is, tailoring your retention strategies to where your audience is in the customer journey as this is another essential consideration for maintaining engagement:

- **Top-of-funnel (TOFU) content**. For awareness-stage content, keeping videos short and emotionally engaging helps capture the interest of a broad audience. These videos should aim to spark curiosity or elicit an emotional response that encourages viewers to learn more.

- **Middle-of-funnel (MOFU)**: For consideration-stage content, the focus should be on building trust and providing valuable information. These videos might include product demonstrations, testimonials or detailed explanations that address the viewer's needs and questions, keeping them engaged as they consider their options. Retention here is earned by providing engaging information that remains highly relevant to the audience's interests and desires.

- **Bottom-of-funnel (BOFU):** For decision-stage content, longer videos that provide in-depth information, case studies or detailed testimonials can be more effective at encouraging retention and driving the required action. These videos should aim to provide all the necessary information that convinces the viewer to make a purchase or take the next steps, and depending on the level of commitment that action will take, someone at this stage of the funnel will likely naturally have a longer attention span.

Forgetful waiters and the power of open loops

Back in the 1920s, psychologist Kurt Lewin noticed something peculiar while dining at his favourite restaurant. The waiters there seemed to have an uncanny ability to remember unpaid orders, but once the tabs were settled, their memory of the details vanished. Intrigued by this phenomenon, Lewin and his colleague Bluma Zeigarnik embarked on a study to understand why this was happening. What they discovered laid the foundation for a concept now known as the Zeigarnik effect, or as it's often referred to today, the open loop effect.

In completing this study, Lewin noticed something intrinsic to human nature: we tend to remember tasks that are incomplete more vividly than those that are completed. Knowledge of this phenomenon can be a powerful tactic in video content creation to make your audience stay engaged longer.

Further research Lewin conducted led to his 'field theory'. This theory explains that an open task creates a sort of 'task tension' in our brains, heightening our focus on ideas related to the unfinished task. This tension is only resolved once the task is completed. Our inherent need to resolve unfinished business is what makes open loops so effective in storytelling and video content.

Think about it: when someone starts a story, don't you feel compelled to hear the ending? Or consider the classic use of cliffhangers in TV serials. These keep viewers on the edge of their seats, eager to tune in next time to see what happens.

The use of open loops plays a critical role in video retention. By understanding and applying this psychological principle, you can create compelling video content that not only grabs attention but also maintains it throughout.

In the context of video content, strategically placing open loops at the beginning or throughout your video can significantly enhance viewer retention. By creating a sense of anticipation and curiosity, you encourage viewers to stick around to see how the story unfolds or how a problem is resolved.

Let's look at some ways that you can effectively implement open loops in your video content:

- **Intriguing introductions:** Start your video with a question or a teaser that hints at the valuable content to come. For example, *What's the one* *mistake most marketers make that costs them thousands of dollars? We'll reveal it in just a moment.*

- **Mid-video hooks:** Use open loops at strategic points in your video to re-engage viewers. For instance, after explaining a concept, you might say, *But what if I told you there's an even easier way to achieve this? We'll get to that soon.*

- **End with teasers:** If your content is part of a series, end your video with a teaser for the next episode. This keeps viewers anticipating the next video and encourages them to subscribe or follow your channel. For example, *In our next video, we'll dive into the advanced techniques that can double your conversion rates. You won't want to miss it.*

- **Open loop visuals:** A clever, and often highly effective way to open loops in your viewer's mind can be with the use of visual cues in your thumbnails or video content. By using unexpected visuals or intriguing objects, you can drive greater retention with your viewers as they keep watching to find out why that object is there, or what is going to happen next. An example of this might be a video thumbnail that shows the aftermath of a slime explosion, for a video describing how to make a slime bomb. Or a video that promises to show you *How to Set Up a Facebook Ad Campaign in 60 seconds* could use a 60-second countdown timer visual on the screen to drive greater retention.

Action: Converting viewers into engaged participants

After successfully capturing attention and maintaining engagement, the final crucial aspect of audience optimisation is driving action. This phase is about guiding your viewers towards a desired result, whether it's:

- Making a purchase
- Subscribing to your channel
- Engaging with your content in another meaningful way.

Understanding how to craft effective calls to action (CTAs) and strategically incorporating them into your videos is essential for achieving your business goals.

First, get super clear about the desired result of your video. After watching the video, what do you want your audience to feel, think and/or do? These desired results guide the entire video creation process and influence how you frame your CTAs.

- **Feel:** Sometimes, the goal of your video is to evoke a specific emotion. This could be happiness, excitement, inspiration, or even urgency. For instance, a motivational video might aim to leave viewers feeling inspired and ready to take action on their goals.
- **Think:** In other cases, you might want your viewers to think differently about a topic or gain new insights. Educational videos, for example, aim to change the

viewer's perspective or increase their understanding of a subject.

- **Do:** The most direct and measurable outcome is getting viewers to take a specific action. This could include subscribing to a channel, signing up for a newsletter, purchasing a product or following your social media accounts.

The different types of CTAs

CTAs can be classified as soft and hard CTAs, and direct and indirect actions, depending on the intensity and nature of the prompt.

Soft CTAs

These encourage viewers to take low-commitment actions such as liking a video, leaving a comment or following a social media account. These actions require minimal effort and are easier for viewers to complete, making them suitable for building engagement and fostering community interactions.

Examples include:

- *'If you enjoyed this video, give it a thumbs up.'*
- *'Leave a comment below with your thoughts.'*

Hard CTAs

These, on the other hand, ask viewers to take more substantial actions that usually involve a higher level of commitment, such as making a purchase or signing up for a service. These actions are crucial for achieving specific business objectives and often require more persuasive messaging.

Examples include:

- *'Sign up for our newsletter to get exclusive updates.'*
- *'Buy now and take advantage of our limited-time offer.'*

Direct actions

Direct CTAs are straightforward commands that tell the viewer exactly what to do. They leave no room for ambiguity and are often used when the desired action is simple and clear.

Examples include:

- *'Click the link below to subscribe.'*
- *'Visit our website to learn more.'*

Indirect actions

These guide viewers towards an action in a more subtle way, often encouraging a transitional step rather than the final goal. These CTAs are useful for nurturing leads and guiding viewers through a funnel.

Examples include:

- *'Download our free guide to learn more.'*
- *'Check out our other videos on this topic.'*

Integrating CTAs seamlessly into your video content ensures that viewers are naturally guided towards the desired action without feeling pressured or overwhelmed.

Here are some strategies for effective CTA integration:

- **Verbal prompts:** Clearly state your CTA towards the end of your video, making it easy for viewers to understand what you want them to do next. For instance, you might say, 'If you found this video helpful, subscribe to our channel for more tips.'

- **Visual cues:** Use on-screen text, buttons or annotations to highlight your CTA. Visual cues can reinforce verbal prompts and provide a clickable element that makes it easy for viewers to take action. For example, a button that says 'Sign Up Now' can be placed prominently on the screen.

- **Contextual relevance:** Ensure that your CTA aligns with the content and context of the video. A tutorial video might have a CTA that guides viewers to related resources or additional tutorials, while a product review video might direct viewers to a purchase link. The CTA should feel like a natural extension of the video's content.

Examples of effective CTAs

Let's look at how successful content creators and businesses incorporate CTAs into their videos:

- **Airbnb:** In their marketing videos, Airbnb effectively uses a combination of soft and hard CTAs to engage viewers and drive conversions. For instance, in a video showcasing a unique property experience, they might start with a soft CTA, encouraging viewers to 'Like' and 'Share' the video to spread the word about the destination. As the video progresses, they transition to a hard CTA, inviting viewers to 'Book your stay today' with a clickable link directing them to the property listing on the Airbnb website.

- **HubSpot:** In their educational videos, HubSpot often includes soft CTAs, encouraging viewers to download free resources or subscribe for more content. These CTAs align with the educational nature of the videos and provide additional value to the viewer.

- **Fitness Influencers:** Many fitness influencers use a mix of soft and hard CTAs. They might start with a soft CTA, asking viewers to like and comment, and then move to a hard CTA, encouraging viewers to sign up for a paid workout program or purchase fitness equipment.

Optimising for the action you want a viewer to take is crucial in overall audience optimisation because it directly translates viewer engagement into tangible business outcomes. By clearly defining and strategically incorporating CTAs into your video content, you guide your audience towards meaningful interactions.

This not only enhances the effectiveness of your video marketing efforts but also ensures that each piece of content contributes to your broader business goals, turning passive viewers into active participants and loyal customers.

Now that you've optimised your video content for attention, retention and action, it's time to turn your efforts to the second element of optimisation—algorithm optimisation.

Algorithm optimisation

Algorithms operate across all distribution platforms, from YouTube and Facebook to Google and Instagram. Year on year these algorithms are becoming more and more sophisticated. As artificial intelligence (AI) continues to develop and drive these algorithms it is simply no longer about trying to 'beat' the algorithm. The primary goal of these algorithms is to determine which content is most relevant to users and display it accordingly. As Video Strategists, our task is to seek to understand and apply the best practices for each platform, keeping their algorithms in mind.

Algorithm optimisation can be simplified into three key factors:

- Relevance
- Volume
- Competition.

These three factors are integral to virtually every platform's algorithm and I'm expecting that they will remain so despite future changes. (But don't hold me to that.)

Relevance

Relevance is the cornerstone of algorithm optimisation. It refers to how closely your content aligns with what the algorithm believes the user wants to see. Several elements influence this relevance:

- **Search queries:** How well your content matches the user's search terms. For example, on YouTube or Google, using relevant words in your video title, video script or description can impact the chance of your video being shown to specific viewers.

- **User behaviour:** Algorithms consider past behaviour and viewing habits. If users have shown interest in similar content, the algorithm is more likely to recommend your video.

- **Geographical relevance:** The location of your audience can affect how content is surfaced. Localised content or content relevant to specific regions or language groups can understandably perform better in those areas.

- **Demographic relevance:** Factors like age, gender and interests, which the platform collects data on, play a role in determining relevance.

Each platform's algorithm aims to show the most relevant content to users at any given time, making it crucial to ensure your videos are highly valuable to your target audience, and therefore more likely to be watched and keeping that audience member on their platform for longer.

Volume

Volume is all about how frequently a type of content is searched for and consumed on a platform. This includes:

- **Search volume:** High search volume (the number of searches for particular keywords) indicates a popular topic. This can drive significant traffic if your content ranks well.

- **Content volume:** The amount of other content available on a particular topic. Platforms might prioritise content types that have proven popular with their audience.

- **Niche versus broad appeal:** Niche content might have a smaller but highly engaged audience, whereas broad appeal content can attract a larger audience. Understanding where your content fits can help in strategising its distribution.

Considering volume is crucial because it helps in understanding the demand for your content. High-demand topics with less competition can be a goldmine, while saturated content niches might require more innovative approaches to stand out.

Competition

Competition refers to the number of other pieces of content vying for the same audience. Algorithms are designed to show the best content to users, which means they filter out what they consider to be lower quality or less relevant content. Here are some considerations:

- **Content saturation:** The more content there is on a particular topic, the harder it is to rank. High competition means you need to ensure your content is exceptionally well-optimised to stand out.

- **Quality indicators:** Engagement metrics like likes, shares, comments and watch time signal to algorithms that your content is valuable. High-quality content that engages users is more likely to be favoured by algorithms.

- **Freshness:** Newer content can sometimes be prioritised over older content, especially if it is timely or relevant to current trends.

By understanding your competition, you can better position your content to stand out. This might involve finding unique angles on popular topics or ensuring your content is of the highest possible quality to outperform competitors.

As we delve deeper into the specifics of algorithm optimisation with regards to some of the key distribution platforms in the following sections, remember that the ultimate goal is to create content that resonates with your audience while also being favoured by the platforms' algorithms. Mastering these elements will significantly enhance the visibility and effectiveness of your video strategy, ensuring your content reaches and engages the right audience.

Optimising for YouTube

Now that we have a solid understanding of optimisation as it applies to both audience and algorithms more generally, it's time to dive into the world of YouTube optimisation specifically. With YouTube's clear dominance as a video distribution platform it is worthwhile for this book to unpack specific tactics and understanding of this platform (relevant at the time of writing) in more detail.

YouTube optimisation is all about playing the long game. Effective optimisation tactics applied here can have lasting value, continuing to deliver returns on your investment for years to come. While platforms like Facebook frequently change their algorithm goals, YouTube's algorithm has consistently aimed to deliver the right content to the right people at the right time. This consistency provides a stable foundation for long-term strategic planning.

It's also essential to recognise that many elements of YouTube optimisation can be adjusted, refined and changed over time. This means that YouTube optimisation is not a one-time task but an ongoing process of tweaking and improving your videos' reach and engagement on the platform.

The three pillars of YouTube algorithm optimisation

The data points that determine ranking in YouTube's algorithm can be categorised into three main areas:

- Metadata
- Social signals
- Platform signals.

Some of these data points are within our control, while others are not. Let's break down each one.

Metadata

Metadata refers to the textual information that accompanies your video or channel. This data helps YouTube understand what your video is about and how to rank it, although this is becoming increasingly less relevant as the role AI plays in the algorithm becomes more heavily weighted.

The primary components of metadata include titles, descriptions, tags and transcripts.

- **Titles:** Your video title is one of the most critical factors in metadata. It should be compelling, concise and include relevant keywords. A well-crafted title not only attracts viewers but also signals to the algorithm what your content is about.

- **Descriptions:** The description box is a valuable space to provide more context about your video. Use this space to include detailed information, relevant keywords and links to other related content. While the algorithm doesn't weigh descriptions as heavily as it once did, they still contribute to overall video SEO and viewer understanding.

- **Tags:** Tags help categorise your video content and improve its discoverability. Use a mix of broad and specific tags that relate to your video's content, ensuring you cover different potential search queries. Also consider using tags to include highly specific terms such as personal names, brand names or common misspellings, as this can be a place for giving the algorithm a few additional signals that may help your content be found. (Note: Tags may soon be going away from the platform, as they are increasingly less relevant but while YouTube still offers them I suggest you use them.)

- **Transcripts:** Adding transcripts or closed captions to your videos can enhance accessibility and improve SEO. Transcripts allow YouTube to better understand the spoken content of your video, which can positively impact your ranking. You can manually add your own transcript, or rely on the automated transcript that YouTube provides. (If using the automated transcript, I would recommend taking some time to fix any errors to maximise the effectiveness of the transcript.)

While metadata used to play a more significant role in YouTube optimisation, advancements in the algorithm and AI have shifted focus towards social signals and platform signals. However, optimising metadata remains an essential foundation for ensuring your content is not only correctly categorised and easily discoverable, but also useful and easy to consume for your audience.

Social signals

Social signals refer to the data YouTube collects based on how audiences interact with your content. These signals include subscribers, shares, links from social media platforms like Facebook and X and inclusion in YouTube playlists. Although you can't directly control these signals, you can influence them by encouraging engagement.

- **Subscribers:** A growing subscriber base indicates to YouTube that your channel provides valuable content. Encourage viewers to subscribe by including clear and compelling CTAs in your videos.

- **Shares:** Shared videos often reach a broader audience, increasing views and engagement. Encourage your viewers to share your content by creating share-worthy videos and reminding them to share at the end of your video.

- **External Links:** Links to your video from external websites and social media platforms can boost its visibility. Promote your videos across your social media channels, and engage with communities that might find your content valuable.

- **Playlists:** When viewers add your videos to their playlists, it signals to YouTube that your content is valuable and worth keeping. Create your own playlists to organise your content and encourage viewers to do the same.

Platform signals

Platform signals are probably the most important factor in determining ranking in the YouTube algorithm today. Here, we're referring to the data points that YouTube collects based on user activity and engagement with your videos. These signals are mostly out of your direct control, but you can influence them through effective content creation and audience engagement strategies.

- **Views:** The number of views your video receives is a fundamental metric. While you can't directly control view counts, you can create high-quality content that encourages viewers to watch and share your videos.

- **Impressions click-through rate:** The click-through rate that your videos receive is a strong indicator to YouTube of the interest in your video to your audience. When YouTube shows your video to someone, that's an 'impression'. The click-through rate is when someone makes a decision to then click on your video. Impressions click-through rate is primarily influenced by the video's thumbnail and title, and works in combination with retention as a key measure of the video's value to an audience.

- **Retention and watch time:** Watch time refers to the total amount of time viewers spend watching your videos. High watch time and good viewer retention indicate to YouTube that your content is engaging and valuable. Aim to create content that keeps viewers engaged throughout the video.

- **Engagement (likes/dislikes, comments, shares):** Engagement metrics such as likes, dislikes, comments and shares are critical indicators of how viewers interact with your content. Encourage viewers to engage with your videos by asking questions, prompting comments and inviting feedback.

- **Session time:** Session time refers to the amount of time a viewer spends on YouTube after watching one of your videos. If your video keeps viewers on the platform longer, it signals to YouTube that your content is valuable. Create engaging content that encourages viewers to explore more of your videos or related content on YouTube, and avoid using language towards the end of your video that might signal to a viewer that the video is ending. Instead structure the end of your videos with the aim to quickly transition a viewer to watching the next video to increase session time.

YouTube's algorithm also considers individual user data points to personalise content recommendations. This includes past viewing behaviour, subscribed channels and demographic information. By understanding and leveraging these factors, you can better tailor your content to meet the needs and interests of your audience.

- **Past viewing behaviour:** YouTube analyses users' past viewing habits to recommend relevant content. By creating videos that align with your audience's interests and viewing patterns, you increase the likelihood of your content being recommended.

- **Subscribed channels:** YouTube considers the channels a user is subscribed to when recommending content. Encourage viewers to subscribe to your channel to ensure your videos appear in their recommended feed.

- **Geographical and demographic data:** Tailor your content to the specific needs and preferences of different geographic and demographic segments. This can help your videos resonate more deeply with targeted audience groups.

Best practices for YouTube optimisation

To optimise your YouTube content effectively, focus on the elements you can control and continuously refine your strategy based on performance data. Here are some best practices:

- **Create high-quality content:** The foundation of any successful YouTube strategy is high-quality content. Ensure your videos are well-produced, engaging and provide value to your audience.

- **Optimise metadata:** Use relevant keywords in your titles, descriptions and tags. Make sure your descriptions are detailed and provide additional context for your videos.

- **Encourage engagement:** Prompt viewers to like, comment, share and subscribe. Engagement signals are crucial for boosting your content's visibility.

- **Promote your videos:** Share your videos on social media, embed them in blog posts and promote them through email newsletters. External promotion can drive traffic and increase visibility.

- **Analyse performance data:** Regularly review your YouTube analytics to understand how your videos are performing. Look for patterns and insights that can inform your content strategy.

- **Experiment and iterate:** Don't be afraid to try new formats, topics and styles. Experimentation can help you discover what resonates best with your audience.

- **Use YouTube tools:** Consider using tools like TubeBuddy and vidIQ to enhance your optimisation efforts. These tools offer features like keyword research, tag suggestions and performance tracking.

An essential aspect of YouTube optimisation is understanding how sophisticated AI technologies, such as Google Vision AI, interpret and categorise video content. Google Vision AI analyses videos frame by frame, understanding not just the spoken words but also the visual elements within the video. This means the algorithm can discern the subject matter more accurately than metadata alone.

To gain insight into how this technology works, you can explore the Google Cloud website, which (as of the time of writing) allows you to test the AI on still images for free. By understanding the capabilities of this technology, you can better align your content creation efforts with the algorithm's analytical processes.

YouTube optimisation is a multifaceted process that requires a strategic approach to metadata, social signals and platform signals. By understanding and leveraging these elements, you can enhance your content's visibility, engagement and overall performance on the platform. Remember, the key to successful YouTube optimisation is to create high-quality, engaging content tailored to your audience's needs and preferences.

While the YouTube algorithm is complex, focusing on audience optimisation first will naturally lead to better algorithmic performance. Keep experimenting, analysing data and refining your strategy to stay ahead in the ever-evolving landscape of YouTube.

In the next section, we will discuss optimisation strategies for other social media platforms, such as with Meta (the parent company for Facebook and Instagram).

Optimising for Meta

The world of video marketing changes rapidly, however as of the time of writing this book, the Meta platforms—Facebook and Instagram—are still heavy hitters in a video distribution strategy. So it's important to understand the current best practices and key tactics for optimising video content on these platforms.

Facebook video optimisation

Note that, while there are similarities between Facebook and Instagram due to their shared ownership and similar algorithm approaches, there are also differences that necessitate tailored strategies for each.

Native video considerations

To optimise for Facebook, consider the format, screen ratio, duration and presence of captions. Currently, a 4x5 (portrait) or 9x16 (vertical) aspect ratio with burnt-in captions is recommended. Start with a highly visual and engaging opening hook, and aim for a total duration of one to three minutes. This setup aligns with typical user behaviour on Facebook, where videos are often watched with the sound off in the news feed or reels platform.

Key distribution optimisation factors

Facebook has revealed several key factors that influence its algorithm:

- Originality
- Viewing behaviours and video attributes
- Loyalty and intent
- Engagement.

Let's break these down.

Originality

Facebook prioritises original content produced directly by the page or through affiliated production companies. The algorithm seeks strong signals of originality, meaning the content should be authentic and valuable, not just a mashup of found footage or re-edited content from elsewhere. However, it is acceptable to reshare your original content from other platforms like YouTube.

Viewing behaviours and video attributes

Facebook aims to promote videos that encourage viewers to watch to the end. Longer videos with a clear storyline are favoured. Retention is key, so create engaging content that holds viewers' attention. Given that many viewers watch with the sound off, ensure your videos are optimised for this behaviour with appropriate screen ratios and captions.

Avoid slideshow-type videos or still images with voiceovers, as well as any clickbait or watch-bait tactics intended to artificially boost watch time.

Loyalty and intent

Building meaningful relationships with your audience is essential. Your video strategy should encourage viewers to return to your page repeatedly. Creating a video series and maintaining a regular publication schedule can foster this loyalty. Additionally, optimise your videos for Facebook search by focusing on elements like video titles and post text.

- **Video titles:** Although not prominently displayed in the news feed, titles work as headlines in the video tab, or paid ads. Optimise titles for search and viewer engagement.

- **Description or post text:** Use authentic, natural language to build intrigue and create an 'open loop' that encourages viewers to watch the video to find the answer. Incorporate short, impactful sentences, emojis where appropriate, and avoid multiple consecutive line breaks.

- **Hashtags:** Include about three relevant hashtags to aid discoverability. Stick to relatively generic hashtags for broader reach.

- **Tags and playlists:** Use relevant tags and create playlists to encourage longer watch times. Group related content into series or topics.

- **Thumbnails:** While most videos autoplay in the news feed, thumbnails are seen on mobile devices, especially when autoplay is turned off due to low battery or poor internet connection. Design thumbnails that are clear and engaging, even on small screens.

Engagement

Create content that naturally encourages authentic engagement through shares, reactions and comments. Avoid engagement bait tactics, as Facebook demotes such content. Instead, foster genuine conversation and interaction. Engage actively in the comments to further the conversation and encourage more engagement.

Instagram video optimisation

For Instagram, many of the optimisation tactics that work on Facebook are applicable. However, there are specific considerations for Instagram's unique environment.

Key differences and best practices for Instagram

- **Duration:** Instagram video (at time of writing) is primarily driven through the Reels platform. As such, videos are restricted to 90-second duration when created via the platform itself but can be up to 15 minutes in duration if uploaded via a third-party tool.

- **Aspect ratio:** Use a 9x16 (vertical) or 4x5 (portrait) aspect ratio, optimised for sound-off viewing.

- **Engagement:** Encourage viewers to click the links in

your bio or send direct messages. This direct interaction can boost your engagement and visibility.

- **Algorithm optimisation:** Foster engagement through comments, likes, DMs and profile visits. These interactions help boost your content in your followers' feeds.

While this section has focused on Instagram video more generally, it's worth noting that Stories and Reels require different strategies. Stories should be short, engaging and interactive, while Reels benefit from trending audio, quick edits and engaging visual effects. We won't dive deeper into these formats here, but keep them in mind as part of your broader Instagram strategy.

Meta platforms like Facebook and Instagram are constantly evolving. What works today might not be as effective tomorrow. Stay updated with platform changes and algorithm updates to ensure your strategies remain relevant.

Optimising for LinkedIn

Creating well optimised videos on LinkedIn involves a strategic approach tailored to the platform's unique audience and technical requirements. To maximise engagement and reach, it's essential to understand the nuances of LinkedIn's video ecosystem and implement best practices designed specifically for this professional network.

Understand LinkedIn's audience and format

LinkedIn's audience is primarily composed of professionals and businesses, making it essential to create content that resonates with this demographic. Unlike more casual platforms, LinkedIn content should balance professionalism with engaging storytelling to capture and retain viewer interest. High-quality production is more crucial here than on platforms such as Facebook and Instagram. So, investing in good lighting, clear audio and professional editing can significantly enhance the perceived value of your videos.

Capture attention early

The first few seconds of your video are critical for capturing attention. Given the professional nature of LinkedIn, start with a compelling hook that is both relevant and intriguing. This could be an interesting fact, a provocative question, or a brief overview of what the viewer will learn. Avoid overly sensational clickbait tactics, as they can undermine your credibility and lead to disengagement.

Design for sound-off viewing

Many LinkedIn users browse their feeds with the sound off, so incorporating captions and on-screen text is essential. Closed captions not only make your videos accessible to a wider audience but also ensure that your message is conveyed even when the sound is muted. Visual storytelling through expressive body language and clear graphics can further enhance engagement.

Encourage interaction

To foster community and engagement, always include a clear CTA at the end of your videos. This could be a prompt to visit your website, download a resource or attend a webinar. Make your CTAs concise and easy to follow, guiding viewers seamlessly to the next step. Additionally, actively participate in the comments section by responding to questions and engaging with viewer feedback to build a stronger connection with your audience. As opposed to other platforms, keeping the conversation going and engagement high in comments is a proven strategy to giving your videos longer life in the LinkedIn feed, and a great way to refresh engagement with content that was posted previously.

Know the technical specifications

Preferred formats for LinkedIn videos include aspect ratios such as 16:9 for desktop or 9:16 for mobile-friendly content. While LinkedIn allows videos up to 10 minutes, keeping your videos between 30 seconds and 5 minutes is generally more effective for maintaining viewer interest. Keep an eye on the shifting landscape on LinkedIn as the platform continues to follow in the footsteps of other platforms with a move towards favouring short-form content too.

LinkedIn's algorithm prioritises content based on relevance, engagement and user activity. By aligning your video content with the interests and needs of your audience, encouraging meaningful interactions, and maintaining an active presence on the platform, you can improve your content's visibility and reach.

Optimising for other platforms

As we round out this chapter on video optimisation, it's important to acknowledge the diversity of social media platforms beyond YouTube, Facebook, Instagram and LinkedIn. Each platform offers unique opportunities and requires tailored strategies to maximise engagement and reach.

- **TikTok** has become a powerhouse in short-form video content, emphasising creativity and viral trends. With its algorithm favouring content that quickly captures attention and drives high engagement, TikTok offers immense potential for brand visibility and audience growth.

- **X** (formerly Twitter) is another valuable platform, particularly for real-time engagement and conversational marketing. Video content on X benefits from being timely, concise and relevant to current trends and discussions. Using hashtags effectively and engaging with trending topics can enhance your video's visibility.

- **Snapchat** continues to be popular among younger demographics. Its ephemeral nature and creative tools make it ideal for creating authentic, behind-the-scenes content that resonates with a youthful audience. Optimising for Snapchat involves leveraging its unique filters, lenses and interactive features.

- **Threads** is a newer platform focused on community-driven, text-based interactions but also supports video content. The key to optimisation here is fostering community engagement and creating content that sparks meaningful conversations.

- **Pinterest** is particularly effective for visually-driven content and discovering new ideas. Video content on Pinterest should be visually appealing, informative, and designed to inspire action, such as trying a new recipe or DIY project.

In summary, while each platform requires its own specific strategies for optimisation, the overarching principles of creating high-quality, engaging content that is tailored to your audience's preferences remain consistent. Staying updated with each platform's best practices and algorithm changes is crucial for maintaining relevance and maximising the impact of your video content across the social media landscape.

By diversifying your approach and leveraging the unique strengths of each platform, you can enhance your overall digital marketing strategy and achieve greater reach and engagement.

But most importantly, focus on optimising for audiences over algorithms, and you'll be on the right track.

BONUS MATERIAL

For downloadable worksheets and resources, head to *engagevideomarketing.com/more*

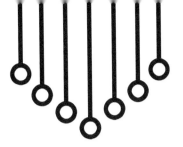

CHAPTER 12

Metrics

Imagine a pilot flying a plane without any instruments. No altimeter, no speedometer, no navigation system—just the view out of the cockpit. It's a clear day, and the pilot can see the horizon, but there's no way to gauge altitude, speed or direction accurately.

Now imagine clouds rolling in, obscuring the view. Without instruments, the pilot has no way to ensure the plane stays on course or avoids potential dangers. This scenario, while extreme, illustrates the critical role of metrics in navigating any complex system, whether it's flying a plane or crafting a video marketing strategy.

Just as a pilot relies on instruments to provide real-time data about the plane's performance and surroundings, a Video Strategist must rely on metrics to understand how their content is performing and make informed decisions. Without these data points, you're essentially flying blind, making guesses rather than informed choices.

The right metrics provide the insights needed to steer your strategy, adjust tactics and achieve your goals.

Legendary business consultant and author Peter Drucker's famous quote, 'What gets measured, gets managed', underscores the importance of data in any strategy. By measuring the right metrics, you can manage your video content more effectively, ensuring it meets your goals and resonates with your audience.

However, you may have also heard Albert Einstein's advice: 'Not everything that can be counted counts, and not everything that counts can be counted.'

As such, the key thing to recognise as a Video Strategist is that you need to be focusing on the metrics that matter most to your objectives, rather than getting bogged down in data overload.

The metrics that matter

To navigate the complex landscape of video marketing, you need to identify and focus on the metrics that align with your strategic goals. These metrics fall into five main buckets:

1. Reach metrics

2. Engagement metrics

3. Conversion metrics

4. Retention metrics

5. Audience metrics.

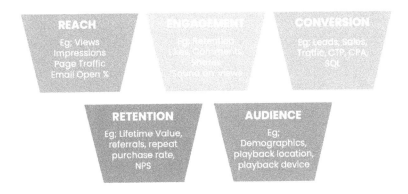

Let's break down each of these metrics buckets one by one and consider which metrics you should be paying attention to at any given time in your video strategy.

1. Reach metrics

These metrics measure how many people have been potentially exposed to your content. Reach is a crucial metric because it provides insight into the breadth of your audience. However, it's important to understand that reach doesn't necessarily equate to engagement or conversion—it's the first step to engaging with your content but an impression or a view doesn't necessarily equate to a valuable audience engagement.

For example, one of the primary reach metrics is the number of views your video receives. However, it's essential to note that not all platforms define a 'view' in the same way. Understanding these differences can help you interpret your reach data more accurately.

- **Facebook, Instagram, X and LinkedIn:** These platforms typically record a view after two continuous seconds of playback, provided at least 50% of the video pixels are in view. This means that even if a viewer doesn't engage deeply with the content, a brief exposure counts as a view.

- **YouTube:** YouTube is more stringent about what constitutes a view. Although YouTube hasn't explicitly disclosed its criteria, it's generally accepted that a view is counted when approximately 30 seconds of the video has been watched. YouTube's algorithm aims to filter out automated views to ensure the view count reflects genuine human interest.

- **Stories (Instagram, Facebook) and TikTok:** For these platforms, a view is counted as soon as the content is rendered on the screen. This means that even a brief glance at the story or TikTok video is considered a view.

Beyond views though, there are other important reach metrics to consider. Some of these include:

- **Impressions:** This metric indicates how many times your content has been displayed, regardless of whether it was clicked or watched. Impressions provide a broader sense of how often your video appears in users' feeds or search results.

- **Page traffic:** This includes the number of visits to your webpage from your video content. High page traffic indicates that your video successfully drives viewers to seek more information on your website.

- **Email open rates:** If you're using video in email marketing, the open rate of your emails can indicate how compelling your video thumbnail or subject line is in encouraging recipients to view your content.

Be aware of vanity metrics

While reach metrics are valuable for understanding how many people see your content, they can often be considered 'vanity metrics'. This term refers to metrics that look impressive on the surface but don't necessarily provide insight into the actual performance or impact of your content. High reach numbers might make your brand appear popular, but without accompanying engagement or conversion metrics (such as likes, comments, shares, and click-throughs or sales), the true value to your business can be limited.

To leverage reach metrics effectively, integrate them with other performance indicators. For instance, a high reach combined with strong engagement metrics suggests that your content is not only being seen but also resonating with your audience. By regularly reviewing and analysing reach data alongside other metrics, you can refine your video marketing strategy to improve both visibility and viewer interaction.

Measuring ROI with reach metrics

Determining the ROI for reach metrics typically involves calculating the cost per thousand impressions (CPM) or cost per view (CPV). These metrics help you understand the financial efficiency of your reach:

- **CPM (Cost per thousand impressions):** This metric tells you how much it costs to achieve one thousand impressions of your video. It's a useful way to gauge the cost-effectiveness of your campaigns in generating visibility.

- **CPV (Cost per view):** This metric indicates the cost of each view your video receives. A lower CPV generally means you're getting more views for your investment, which can be indicative of effective targeting and compelling content.

Note: determining financial ROI metrics can be directly reported via your ads manager when using paid content strategies, however the same calculations can apply for organic content. The challenge here is initially calculating the related cost of producing and managing a piece of content online. Once you have that cost clear then you can calculate the organic ROI. For example, what did an organic instagram reel cost you to produce and publish both in production costs and time? Take that number and divide it by the number of views the content received. Now you have your organic CPV.

2. Engagement Metrics

While reach metrics provide valuable insights into how many people have seen your content, engagement metrics offer a deeper understanding of how your audience interacts with it. For many strategic goals, these metrics are more valuable than reach because higher engagement often directly correlates with greater effectiveness in moving people to take the desired action.

Viewer retention and watch time

One of the most critical engagement metrics to track is viewer retention or watch time. This metric indicates how long viewers actually watch your video, either in total time or as a percentage of the video's length. High retention rates suggest that your content is engaging and relevant to your audience, keeping them interested from start to finish. Platforms like YouTube and Facebook provide detailed analytics on viewer retention, allowing you to identify drop-off points and understand which parts of your video are most engaging.

Understanding viewer retention helps you make informed decisions about your content strategy. For example, if you notice that viewers consistently drop off at a certain point, you can analyse that segment to determine why it isn't resonating and make adjustments in future videos.

Other key engagement metrics

In addition to viewer retention, several other metrics are crucial for measuring engagement:

- **Likes, shares and comments:** These metrics indicate active audience participation and interaction with your content. A high number of likes, shares and comments suggests that viewers find your content valuable and engaging enough to interact with and share with their networks.
- **Session time:** This measures the total time a user spends engaging with your content or platform during

a single visit. Longer session times indicate that viewers are not only watching your video but are also exploring additional content.

- **Time on page:** This metric shows how long viewers spend on the webpage where your video is embedded. Increased time on page often correlates with higher engagement levels, as viewers are likely consuming more of your content.

- **Sound-on views:** This metric is particularly relevant for platforms where videos autoplay without sound. Sound-on views indicate that viewers found your content engaging enough to turn on the sound, suggesting a deeper level of interest and engagement.

Measuring ROI for engagement

Determining the ROI for engagement involves metrics such as Cost per Click (CPC) or Retention Rate (%) or in some cases metrics such as the Thumbstop Ratio (TSR).

- **Cost per Click (CPC):** This metric tracks the cost of each click generated by your video content. CPC is particularly useful for assessing the effectiveness of your video in driving traffic to your website or landing page.

- **Retention Rate (%):** This is a metric that provides insights into how long viewers are engaged with a video and at what point they start losing interest or stop watching altogether. It is usually reported as an average percentage viewed with respect to the total length of the video.

- **Thumbstop Ratio (TSR):** A somewhat custom metric depending on the platform but a super valuable one to consider for paid ad creative. TSR is a measure of the percentage of impressions that made it to a certain part of your video. On Meta Ads, that is three seconds. On TikTok, that is six seconds.

Engagement metrics are invaluable because they provide insight into how well your content resonates with your audience. High engagement levels typically indicate that your content is effective at capturing and maintaining viewers' interest, encouraging them to interact and take action. These metrics are essential for refining your video marketing strategy, ensuring that your content not only reaches a broad audience but also drives meaningful interactions and conversions.

3. Conversion Metrics

Once you have effectively reached and engaged your audience, the next crucial step in your video strategy is to drive conversions. Conversion metrics are arguably the most critical indicators of success from a business perspective. These metrics measure when someone takes the desired action after watching your video, providing tangible evidence of the video's impact on your business goals.

Let's explore the various conversion metrics in detail and understand how they contribute to a successful video marketing strategy.

While reach and engagement metrics indicate how many people saw and interacted with your content, conversion metrics show whether these interactions led to meaningful actions, such as making a purchase or signing up for a lead magnet. High conversion rates suggest that your videos are effectively persuading viewers to take the desired action, thereby delivering a measurable ROI.

Key conversion metrics

The key conversion metrics are:

- **Sales:** This metric measures the revenue generated directly from your video content. For ecommerce businesses, tracking sales conversions from video ads or product demos can provide clear insights into the effectiveness of your video marketing efforts.

- **New leads:** This metric tracks the number of potential customers who have expressed interest in your product or service after watching your video. New leads can be captured through form fills, newsletter sign-ups or webinar registrations.

- **Lead quality:** Beyond the quantity of leads, it's essential to measure the quality of those leads. High-quality leads are more likely to convert into paying customers. Metrics such as lead scoring or tracking the progression of leads through the sales funnel can provide insights into lead quality.

- **Conversion rate:** This metric measures the percentage of viewers who take the desired action after watching your video. For instance, if 1000 people watch your video and 100 of them make a purchase, your conversion rate is 10%. A higher conversion rate indicates that your video content is compelling and persuasive.

- **Traffic:** Tracking the amount of traffic driven to your website from your video content is another important metric. This can include direct traffic from clickable links within the video or from accompanying text and social media posts.

- **Click to Purchase Rate:** This metric measures the percentage of viewers who click on a CTA and then complete a purchase. For example, if 500 viewers click on a product link in your video and 50 of them make a purchase, your click to purchase rate is 10%. This metric is crucial for understanding the effectiveness of your CTAs and the overall purchase process.

Measuring ROI for conversion metrics

To determine the ROI of your video marketing efforts, it's essential to calculate the cost associated with achieving each conversion. Two of the most common metrics for this purpose are:

- **Cost Per Acquisition (CPA):** CPA measures the cost incurred to acquire a new customer through your video marketing efforts. It's calculated by dividing the total cost of the campaign by the number of conversions. A lower CPA indicates a more cost-effective campaign.

- **Cost Per Lead (CPL):** CPL measures the cost of generating a new lead. It's calculated by dividing the total campaign cost by the number of leads generated. Similar to CPA, a lower CPL signifies a more efficient lead generation process.

Effectively utilising conversion metrics involves continuously monitoring and analysing the data to refine your video strategy. For instance, if you notice that a particular video has a high view rate but low conversions, you may need to reassess the video's CTA or the relevance of the content to your target audience. Split testing (A/B testing) different versions of your videos can also help identify which elements drive higher conversion rates.

Conversion metrics provide actionable insights that allow you to optimise your video content for better performance. By focusing on these metrics, you can ensure that your video marketing efforts translate into real, measurable business outcomes.

4. Retention Metrics

As a Video Strategist familiar with the Full Funnel Video Strategy Framework™, you're probably starting to see a trend here: metrics play a crucial role at every stage of the customer journey.

The next set of metrics to consider are retention metrics, which focus on what happens with a customer after the sale. Retention metrics provide insights into the longevity and quality of the relationship between your business and its customers. They help gauge how well you are retaining customers, encouraging repeat purchases and fostering loyalty and advocacy.

Key retention metrics

Retention metrics track various aspects of customer behaviour and satisfaction post-purchase. They provide a comprehensive view of customer loyalty and the ongoing value that each customer brings to your business. By understanding and improving these metrics, you can enhance customer satisfaction, reduce churn, and increase lifetime value. The key retention metrics are:

- **Lifetime Value (LTV):** The key metric for retention is usually Lifetime Value, which measures the total income generated by each customer over the duration of their relationship with your business. LTV is a crucial indicator of customer loyalty and advocacy. A higher LTV suggests that customers are not only staying longer but also making repeat purchases and engaging deeply with your brand.

- **Repeat Purchase Rate:** This metric tracks how often customers return to make additional purchases. A high repeat purchase rate indicates strong customer satisfaction and a compelling reason for customers to come back.

- **Customer Churn Rate:** The churn rate measures the percentage of customers who stop doing business with you over a specific period. A lower churn rate indicates better customer retention. Identifying factors that contribute to churn can help you implement strategies to improve customer satisfaction and loyalty.

- **Referrals:** This metric tracks the number of new customers acquired through word-of-mouth referrals from existing customers. High referral rates often indicate strong customer satisfaction and trust in your brand.

- **Net Promoter Score (NPS):** NPS measures customer satisfaction and loyalty by asking customers how likely they are to recommend your product or service to others. You know the ones: 'On a scale of 1 to 10 how likely are you to recommend this salmon pâté to someone?' A high NPS indicates strong customer loyalty and advocacy.

- **Customer Complaints:** Tracking customer complaints can provide insights into areas where your product or service may be falling short. Addressing these complaints effectively can lead to improved customer satisfaction and retention.

Measuring ROI for Retention Metrics

To measure the ROI for content aimed at improving retention, it's essential to assign a dollar value to LTV. This involves calculating the average revenue generated per customer and the average duration of the customer relationship. By understanding LTV, you can assess the financial impact of your retention strategies and make informed decisions about where to invest your resources.

For example, if your average customer spends $100 per month and stays with your business for two years, their LTV would be $2,400. If a particular video campaign costs $10,000 but results in a 10% increase in LTV across your customer base, the ROI of that campaign can be substantial.

Retention metrics are invaluable for refining your video strategy and ensuring that your content continues to deliver value long after the initial purchase. By focusing on these metrics, you can create videos that address common customer pain points, celebrate customer milestones and encourage repeat purchases and referrals.

For instance, personalised thankyou videos or instructional content that helps customers get the most out of their purchases can significantly enhance customer satisfaction and loyalty. Similarly, showcasing customer success stories and testimonials can build trust and encourage new customers to make a purchase.

5. Audience Metrics

The final bucket of metrics is what I refer to as audience metrics. Unlike other metrics that measure specific actions taken by viewers, audience metrics focus on who the viewers are. These metrics provide valuable insights into the demographics and behaviours of the audience engaging with your videos. Understanding these metrics helps refine your video strategy and ensures your content resonates with the intended audience.

Audience metrics are crucial because they allow you to see who is interacting with your content. By analysing this data, you can determine if your videos are reaching the right people and identify any unexpected audiences that might present new opportunities. These insights can guide adjustments to your strategy, ensuring your videos are tailored to engage the most relevant and valuable viewers.

Key audience metrics

Most platforms provide detailed demographic data about your audience. This includes:

- **Geographical location:** Knowing where your viewers are located helps tailor content to regional preferences and time zones. For instance, if you discover a significant portion of your audience is from a specific country or city, you might create content that caters to regional interests or cultural nuances.

- **Age:** Understanding the age distribution of your viewers can inform the tone, style and topics of your videos. For example, content aimed at younger audiences might use more contemporary references and a faster pace, while content for older audiences might be more informative and measured.

- **Playback locations:** This metric indicates where your videos are being viewed, such as on your website, social media platforms or embedded in external sites. Understanding playback locations helps you optimise your distribution strategy to focus on platforms that drive the most engagement.

- **Playback devices:** Knowing which devices your audience uses to watch your videos (e.g. mobile phones, tablets, desktops) can influence how you format and produce your content. For instance, if a large portion of your audience watches on mobile devices, ensuring your videos are mobile-friendly with appropriate aspect ratios and clear, concise messaging is crucial.

- **Traffic sources:** This metric reveals how viewers find your videos, such as through search engines, social media shares, direct links or referrals from other websites. Understanding traffic sources helps you identify the most effective channels for promoting your content and can inform your overall marketing strategy.

By paying close attention to audience metrics, you can continuously refine your video strategy to better meet the needs and preferences of your viewers. For example, if you notice a growing number of viewers from a particular demographic, you might decide to create more content tailored to that group. Alternatively, if you find that a significant portion of your audience discovers your videos through social media, you could invest more in social media marketing and engagement.

Audience metrics also help you identify gaps in your strategy. If you intended to reach a specific demographic but the data shows you're not engaging that group, you can adjust your content and distribution methods accordingly. This iterative process ensures your video marketing efforts are aligned with your strategic goals and audience needs.

The challenge with audience metrics is that not all distribution platforms provide the same level of insight into this data as we might like. YouTube Analytics is currently a clear winner here, with deep insight and data into the viewing audience, however other platforms don't yet give the level of data we might sometimes require for the right insight.

Regardless of the depth of data you are able to access, paying attention to your audience insights is invaluable for tailoring your content to better resonate with your target audience and for discovering new opportunities to expand your reach. By integrating audience metrics into your video strategy, you can create more effective, targeted and engaging content that drives meaningful results for your business.

Aligning metrics with video strategy goals

As a Video Strategist, understanding how the five metrics buckets—Reach, Engagement, Conversion, Retention, and Audience—align with your video strategy goals is crucial. This knowledge allows you to provide the best advice and make informed decisions to optimise video performance and achieve desired outcomes.

Let's explore how these metrics align with the goals of brand positioning, social engagement, conversion and delight.

Brand Positioning

The first goal, brand positioning, is all about visibility. Here, the objective is to get as many eyeballs on your video as possible to ensure that your brand message reaches a broad audience. **Therefore, the metrics that matter most are from the reach and engagement buckets.**

Reach metrics, such as impressions and views, help determine how many people have seen your video. These metrics provide a quantitative measure of your content's visibility. Engagement metrics, such as viewer retention and watch time, indicate how well your content is capturing and maintaining audience interest.

Social Engagement

For the goal of social engagement, the focus shifts to building and nurturing relationships with your audience. Here, **engagement metrics are paramount**. These metrics help assess how well your video content is fostering connections and encouraging interactions with your viewers.

Key metrics to monitor include likes, shares, comments and session time. High engagement suggests that your content resonates with viewers and effectively builds the 'know, like, and trust' factor crucial for developing lasting relationships.

Conversion

When the goal shifts to conversion, the focus is on driving specific actions that lead to tangible business outcomes. It's no surprise then that **conversion metrics are critical here**, as they measure the effectiveness of your video content in persuading viewers to take desired actions, such as making a purchase, signing up for a newsletter or requesting more information.

Important conversion metrics include sales, new leads, lead quality, conversion rate, traffic and click-to-purchase rate.

These metrics provide clear evidence of your video content's impact on your business goals. By analysing conversion data, you can identify which videos drive the most conversions and optimise your strategy accordingly.

Delight

The goal of delight focuses on retention and building long-term relationships with your customers. **Retention metrics are essential here**, as they measure how well your video content keeps customers engaged and encourages repeat business. These metrics provide insights into customer loyalty, satisfaction and advocacy.

By focusing on retention metrics, you can create video content that deepens customer relationships, enhances satisfaction and drives long-term business growth.

As a Video Strategist, your role involves looking back at the data to measure video effectiveness and using those insights to inform future strategies. For example, if you notice higher engagement with interview-style videos, you can create more of that content. If Google Analytics shows more traffic to a sales page from Facebook than LinkedIn, you can prioritise Facebook in your distribution strategy.

Metrics also help connect online data to offline behaviours. By tracking sales, phone enquiries, and new customer acquisitions, you can gauge the real-world impact of your video marketing efforts.

Ultimately, the goal is to identify the metrics that matter for each video and implement procedures to track and analyse this data effectively. By aligning metrics with your strategic goals, you can optimise your video content to drive meaningful results and achieve business success.

Understanding attribution

When it comes to metrics, understanding the above is good, but understanding the concept and power of attribution will allow you to truly harness the power of your data.

Attribution modelling allows you to identify which touchpoints in the customer journey are most influential in driving conversions. This deeper insight is crucial for making informed, data-driven decisions about your video strategy, particularly when you are introducing any paid amplification into the mix.

The basics of attribution

Attribution models help us understand which marketing channels and touchpoints are contributing to conversions. There are three primary types of attribution models: first-touch attribution, last-touch attribution and mulititouch attribution.

First-touch attribution

In a first-touch attribution model, 100% of the value of the conversion is assigned to the first marketing touchpoint or the place where the customer first entered your marketing funnel. This model gives credit to the initial acquisition channel, assuming it had the most significant impact on the customer's decision to enter the funnel. However, it ignores any subsequent interactions that may have influenced the customer's journey.

For instance, if a customer first discovers your brand through a Facebook ad and later interacts with various other channels before making a purchase, the first-touch attribution model would credit the Facebook ad for the conversion. This model is useful for understanding which channels are most effective at generating initial interest.

Last-touch attribution

On the other hand, last-touch attribution assigns 100% of the value of the conversion to the last action or touchpoint that a customer had prior to making the conversion. This model credits the final interaction that led directly to the purchase, assuming it had the most significant impact on the customer's decision to convert.

For example, if a customer interacts with several touchpoints but makes the final purchase after clicking on a Google search ad, the last-touch attribution model would credit the Google ad for the conversion. This model is useful for understanding which channels are most effective at closing sales.

Multi-touch attribution

A more valuable but much more complex model is multi-touch attribution, where a percentage of value is assigned to each touchpoint across the full funnel by mapping out and tracking the customer journey that led to a conversion. This model provides a more holistic view of how different touchpoints contribute to the final conversion.

Multi-touch attribution can be implemented in various ways, such as:

- **Linear attribution:** Every touchpoint receives equal credit.
- **Time decay attribution:** Touchpoints closer to the conversion receive more credit.
- **Position-based attribution:** The first and last touchpoints receive the most credit, with the remaining credit distributed among the middle touchpoints.

Implementing attribution models

Attribution can be determined by utilising a combination of analytics platforms such as Google Analytics and Tag Manager, in combination with platform analytics such as Facebook Analytics, YouTube Analytics and shopping cart analytics. These tools help track customer interactions and provide data to assign value accurately to different touchpoints.

Choosing the right attribution model

Selecting the right attribution model for your organic or paid video strategy depends on various factors, including your marketing goals, the complexity of your customer journey and the resources available for data collection and analysis.

- **First-touch attribution:** is beneficial when your primary goal is to understand which channels are most effective at generating initial awareness and interest. If your brand is struggling to attract new leads, focusing on first-touch attribution can help identify the most impactful acquisition channels.

- **Last-touch attribution:** is useful when your primary goal is to understand which channels are most effective at driving conversions. If your brand excels at attracting leads but needs to improve conversion rates, focusing on last-touch attribution can help identify the most effective closing channels.

- **Multi-touch attribution:** provides the most comprehensive view of the customer journey by accounting for all touchpoints. This model is ideal for brands with complex marketing mixes and longer sales cycles, where multiple interactions contribute to the final conversion. However, it requires robust data collection and analysis capabilities.

Practical considerations when determining attribution

Implementing multi-touch attribution can be resource-intensive, requiring detailed mapping of the customer journey and sophisticated analytics tools. For many businesses, starting with a simpler model like first-touch or last-touch attribution can provide valuable insights without overwhelming complexity.

A good starting point is to choose either first-touch or last-touch, depending on where your brand needs the most improvement across the marketing funnel. If your brand is effective at generating initial interest but needs to improve conversion rates, last-touch attribution might be more valuable. Conversely, if your brand excels at closing sales but needs to attract more leads, first-touch attribution could be more beneficial.

Understanding attribution at least at a fundamental level is crucial for Video Strategists aiming to evaluate and optimise their video marketing efforts. Whether you're focusing on paid amplification or organic strategies, choosing the right attribution model helps identify the most effective channels and touchpoints, enabling data-driven decisions that enhance overall marketing performance. By leveraging analytics tools and adopting a strategic approach to attribution, you can ensure your video strategy is driving meaningful results and contributing to your business goals.

BONUS MATERIAL

For downloadable worksheets and resources, head to *engagevideomarketing.com/more*

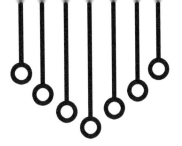

CHAPTER 13

Production

The seventh and final element of an effective video strategy is production. And for those reading this book who identify as video producers or content creators, this seems like a bit of a backwards approach as typically our sole focus is on the nuances of production itself—how to bring a video concept to life, the technical approach, camera choices, whether to use interviews or direct-to-camera pieces, and so forth.

However, the paradigm shift for Video Strategists is recognising that decision-making around production should be the last step in the strategic process.

To be successful with video marketing, we need to make strategic decisions about audience, goals, content, distribution, optimisation and metrics first and allow those decisions to inform the production process.

A strategy-based production process

Traditionally, video producers and content creators have focused heavily on content production. This involves creating video content to communicate a particular message. Sometimes, there might be some strategic decision-making before production, such as a creative brief from a marketing agency or a pre-production planning session with a client to clarify the message before creating the script or treatment. Despite this, our role has traditionally been centred around content production.

To execute an effective video strategy, however, two other critical processes must also take place to ensure that the content produced is successful and gets results:

- Strategy design
- Strategy management.

I call the intersection of these three things the **Video Marketing Sweet Spot**.

Many companies focus mostly on **content production—** creating quality videos. But content creation is just one piece. production should follow on from strategic decisions made about audience, goals, optimisation etc.

Some companies may even be starting to consider the right **strategic approach**. They may even go so far as to do some sort of strategy design process, and document a plan for their videos prior to getting the content produced. That's a great

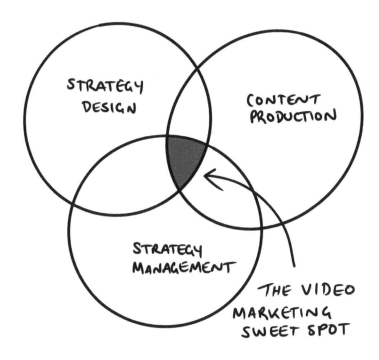

start; however only covers two aspects required for effective video marketing.

Effective video needs ongoing **strategy management** as well: distribution, optimisation, analytics interpretation, encouraging interaction, revising and refining. Too often companies neglect the strategy management phase entirely. They may simply publish a video and then leave it to languish in a digital no-man's land or in other cases the responsibility for the management of the content lies with another department, or an outsourced social media manager who is disconnected from the overall strategy in play.

When all three phases work together, you end up with a high-impact video marketing engine running on all cylinders. Seamless alignment between strategy, production and management is the video marketing sweet spot.

Think of the three elements of the video marketing sweet spot as the legs on a three-legged stool. If any one of these legs are missing, or wobbly, then the stool is unlikely to stand up. However, if all three of these legs are well-formed and strong, then you've got a solid foundation for video marketing (and a solid stool too).

As Video Strategists, it's our role to ensure that all three aspects are handled well with each and every video.

With a strategic approach to video, we recognise that production is the last element to focus on in the strategy design phase. Once the strategy has been designed, we move into the content production phase to produce the video. After production, we transition into the strategy management phase to implement the decisions regarding distribution, optimisation and metrics. This involves doing everything necessary to ensure the video's success online. When you start with a clear strategy, your production efforts are guided by well-defined goals and a deep understanding of your audience.

Integrating strategy and production

Here's how to integrate strategy into the production process effectively structured around the seven elements you're now super familiar with:

- **Audience-centric production:** The first strategic element is understanding your audience. Knowing who your viewers are and what they care about informs the tone, style and content of the video. For example, a video aimed at young adults might use a more casual and energetic style, while a video for professionals might be more polished and formal.

- **Goal-oriented content:** Your goals dictate the purpose of the video. Are you aiming to build brand awareness, engage your audience, drive conversions or retain customers? Each goal requires a different approach in production. For instance, a brand awareness video might focus on storytelling and emotional connection, while a conversion-focused video might highlight product features and include a strong CTA.

- **Content strategy alignment:** The content of your video should align with your overall content strategy. This involves planning the message, structure and key points of the video to ensure it fits within your broader marketing efforts. It's about creating content that not only stands alone but also supports your other marketing activities.

- **Distribution platform considered production:** When a strategic approach is taken, the intended distribution and publication platforms for any piece of video content is locked in before production takes place. As such, production and post-production style of the content can be customised to suit the distribution platform's native style.

- **Optimised production techniques:** Production techniques should be chosen based on the distribution channels and optimisation strategies identified earlier. For example, if your video will be primarily viewed on mobile devices, you might opt for vertical video formats. If SEO is a priority, you'll need to ensure your video includes relevant keywords in the script and metadata.

- **Metrics-driven adjustments:** Finally, metrics from previous videos should inform your production process. If data shows that your audience prefers shorter videos, you can adjust your production plans accordingly. If certain types of videos, like interviews or tutorials, perform better, you can focus on creating more of that content.

A continuous cycle of improvement

The strategic approach to video production is not a one-time effort. It's a continuous cycle of planning, producing, implementing, and then analysing the results to inform future strategies. This iterative process ensures that your video marketing efforts are always improving and adapting to the needs of your audience and the goals of your business.

After each video is produced and distributed, you gather data on its performance. This data helps you understand what worked well and what didn't, providing valuable insights for the next round of strategy design. By continuously refining your approach based on real-world results, you ensure that each new video is more effective than the last.

Balancing quantity and budget

One of the key benefits of planning video content strategically is the ability to make deliberate decisions about budget and production approach. It's important to recognise that across a Full Funnel Video Strategy Framework™, different stages will require varying levels of production effort, resulting in different budgets and approaches.

The Inverse Rule of Strategic Production

To better understand this concept, we can refer to what I call the Inverse Rule of Strategic Production. This rule helps guide the allocation of budget and resources across the customer journey, ensuring that investments are made where they can be most effective. The rule suggests that higher budget productions should be allocated to top-of-funnel content, while lower budget, personalised videos should be focused on as you move towards conversion and delight.

The Cost vs Quantity Inverse Rule

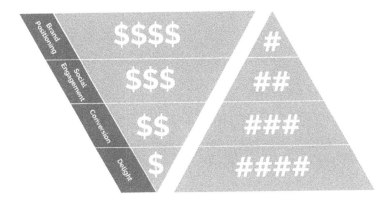

When you reference the above diagram, the cost versus quantity inverse rule illustrates this concept clearly: at the top of the funnel, the budget is high, but the quantity of videos is low. As we move down the funnel towards conversion and delight, the budget decreases while the quantity of videos increases.

Top of Funnel: Brand positioning

At the top of the funnel, where the goal is brand positioning, there is usually a requirement for higher budgets but fewer videos. The objective here is to create a powerful impression and engage a cold audience, pulling them into the funnel. High-quality production values are crucial for this stage because the content needs to represent the brand in the best possible light.

Typically, this might involve producing a highly polished brand story video and a few compelling client story videos. Investing heavily at this stage pays off by establishing a strong brand image that resonates with the target audience. A well-produced brand video can serve as the cornerstone of your marketing efforts, creating a lasting impact and building brand recognition.

Middle of Funnel: Social engagement

In the middle of the funnel, the focus shifts to social engagement. Here, you still want to maintain good production quality, but the quantity of videos increases. The content should aim to build relationships and engage viewers by providing value and fostering trust.

At this stage, producing a series of videos that answer common questions, showcase product benefits or highlight customer testimonials can be effective. While these videos should still look professional, they do not need to have the same high production value as the top-of-funnel content. Allocating a moderate budget to create a larger volume of engaging videos helps keep your audience engaged and moving through the funnel.

Bottom of Funnel: Conversion

As we move to the bottom of the funnel, where the goal is conversion, the quantity of videos needed increases further. Each product or service may require its own dedicated video to address specific customer concerns and encourage purchases.

Here, the focus is on providing clear, concise and persuasive content that drives viewers to take action. Videos at this stage can often be produced at a lower cost, leveraging tools like smartphones or simple editing software to create effective content. The emphasis is on the message rather than high production value. For example, product demos, explainer videos and customer testimonials can be highly effective at driving conversions without breaking the bank.

Post-Purchase: Delight

The final stage, delight, is all about nurturing the customer relationship post-purchase. This stage potentially requires the highest quantity of videos, but with the lowest production costs. The goal is to personalise the customer experience and reinforce their decision to choose your brand.

Personalised videos, such as thank you messages, product usage tips and follow-up communications, can be created quickly and affordably using tools like smartphones or webcam recordings. These videos help maintain a strong connection with customers, encourage repeat purchases and foster loyalty.

This inverse rule for production is extremely helpful when positioning a video strategy for a client. It helps clients understand how to allocate their budget effectively and demonstrates how the Full Funnel Video Strategy Framework™ can be successful regardless of the size of the business.

For instance, a small business might invest a significant portion of their budget into a single, high-quality brand video to attract attention and establish credibility. Meanwhile, they can use lower-budget, high-quantity videos to maintain engagement and drive conversions. On the other hand, a larger business with more resources can produce a series of high-quality videos for each stage of the funnel, ensuring a consistent and professional presence throughout the customer journey.

By strategically planning video production with the inverse rule in mind, you can ensure that your video marketing efforts are both cost-effective and impactful, driving meaningful results for your business.

Professional production or DIY?

As a Video Strategist, we know the importance of producing the right video for the right purpose in the right way. As such, understanding where different styles and approach to video production fits into your strategy is crucial for maximising the impact of your video content while staying within budget constraints.

The role of professional production

Professional video production often involves higher costs but delivers superior quality and polish. This approach is particularly valuable at the top of the funnel, where the goal is brand positioning. At this stage, your objective is to create a powerful impression and engage a cold audience, pulling them into the funnel. High-quality production values are usually most important for this stage because the content needs to represent the brand in the best possible light.

Typically, this might involve producing a highly polished brand story video and a few compelling client story videos. Investing heavily at this stage pays off by establishing a strong brand image that resonates with the target audience. A well-produced brand video can serve as the cornerstone of your marketing efforts, creating a lasting impact and building brand recognition.

The place for lower budget content

As we move down the funnel, the need for high production value decreases, and the focus shifts to quantity and personalisation. Middle-of-the-funnel content, aimed at social engagement, still benefits from good production quality but doesn't necessarily require the same level of investment as top-of-funnel content. Here, you can use a mix of professional and DIY or lower budget content to maintain engagement and build relationships.

For conversion-focused content at the bottom of the funnel, quantity often outweighs the need for high production value. Videos at this stage can be produced using simple tools like smartphones or basic editing software. The emphasis is on clear, persuasive messaging that drives viewers to take action, rather than on high production value.

The value of user-generated content (UGC) and brand-generated content (BGC)

Adding to the cost versus quantity inverse rule concept, we need to consider the growing importance of both UGC and BGC. Encouraging content created by users and customers, as well as raw, behind-the-scenes footage produced by staff members, can significantly enhance a video strategy regardless of company size.

Many large corporations have seen success with campaigns featuring behind-the-scenes, rough and raw footage filmed on smartphones. This type of content provides an authentic glimpse into the business, giving it a sense of realness and transparency. Similarly, UGC, where customers share their experiences and testimonials, creates relatable and trustworthy content that resonates well with potential customers.

This approach highlights the significant value in producing video content that is native to the distribution platform. It appears in a way that audiences expect and engage with, feeling more like content shared by a friend than by a brand. Embracing both UGC and BGC not only diversifies the content mix but also fosters a deeper connection with the audience, leveraging authenticity and relatability to stand out in a crowded digital landscape.

Embracing a media company mindset

For many businesses, embracing a media company mindset is essential. It is no longer enough for companies to simply deliver their products or services while relying on sporadic marketing campaigns to drive the business forward. Instead, companies need to embrace content creation, digital communication and value design across the entire organisation—not just the marketing department.

Video is no longer something that gets created a few times a year, wrapped up in a specific campaign. Rather, video content should be created almost every day or every week and used in various ways across the full funnel. Every employee should potentially be empowered to create video content daily, either for marketing and prospecting, for one-to-one communication and relationship building, or for internal communications to build team and company culture from the inside.

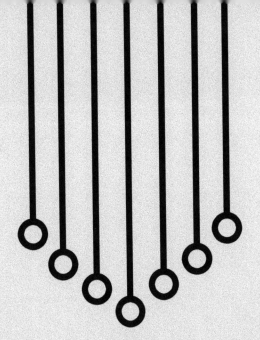

PART 3
Video Strategy in Practice

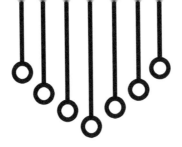

CHAPTER 14

Three powerful video strategy tools

Up until now, we've developed a comprehensive understanding of the elements that make up an effective video strategy. Now it's time to put that knowledge to work.

Over the coming chapters, we will transition from theory to practice by providing you with practical templates, tools and frameworks that you can immediately apply in your business or with your clients. This chapter aims to equip you with actionable strategies to enhance your video marketing efforts and achieve tangible results.

First, we'll introduce the **7-minute Video Marketing Strategy,** a distilled version of the comprehensive strategy we've detailed throughout this book. This quick and efficient planning process will help you outline a strategic approach to video marketing in just seven minutes (give or take), ensuring that even with limited time, you can create a robust strategy.

Then, I'll share with you a powerful template designed to ensure each video you create is strategic in nature and set up for success. The **One Page Video Strategy Canvas** template will guide you through the essential elements of strategic video creation, from defining your audience and goals to planning content and distribution.

Finally, we'll explore **The Simple 7**, a straightforward video strategy content plan that any business can adopt without a significant budget. The Simple 7 offers a practical approach to video content creation that focuses on seven easy-to-produce video types, each mapped to a specific stage of the customer journey. This plan demonstrates that effective video marketing doesn't require a hefty budget but rather a strategic approach to content creation.

Finally, we'll go through some case studies that will show you the principles covered in this book in action.

By the end of this section, you'll have a suite of practical tools at your disposal, enabling you to implement and manage effective video strategies that drive engagement, conversions and customer loyalty. And some inspiration to ensure you feel this is something you can do!

Let's dive in and transform the concepts we've learnt into actionable strategies that deliver real results.

BONUS MATERIAL

For downloadable worksheets and resources, head to *engagevideomarketing.com/more*

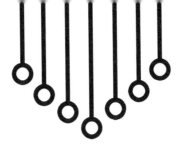

CHAPTER 15

The 7-minute Video Marketing Strategy

Creating a video marketing strategy for your business doesn't need to be complicated. In fact, the detailed understanding you've now developed by reading this book can quite simply be distilled down into just seven key decisions. To make this process simple enough for any business owner to go through, I've developed a streamlined approach that I call the 7-minute Video Marketing Strategy.

This process is based on seven key decisions and can be completed in as little as seven minutes.

Step 1: Identify your target audience (1 minute)

Understanding who you are trying to reach is crucial for creating content that resonates with them. Demographic data such as age, gender and location are a good starting point, but to truly engage your audience, you need to dig deeper into psychographics. Ask yourself questions about their pain points, motivations and what keeps them up at night. By understanding these aspects, you can tailor your content to address their specific needs and interests, making your videos more impactful and relevant.

Step 2: Define your goals (1 minute)

Next, you need to determine what you want to achieve with your video marketing efforts. Marketing is about moving people to take action, so you need to be clear about what action you want your audience to take after watching your video. This could be to feel something different about your brand, think about a new idea or concept, or take a specific action such as signing up for a newsletter or making a purchase. Aligning these objectives with your overall business goals ensures that your video marketing strategy contributes to your company's success.

Step 3: Determine what content your audience needs from you (1 minute)

Once you know who you are targeting and what you want to achieve, the next step is to determine what information or message your audience needs to hear. This involves developing a content plan that outlines the key points you want to communicate. Focus on providing value through education, information and inspiration. Think about what your audience needs to understand, learn or believe in order to take the desired action. This step is crucial for creating content that not only captures attention but also drives engagement and action.

Step 4: Choose your distribution channels (1 minute)

With a clear understanding of your audience and goals, the next decision is about distribution. Where will you publish your videos to reach your target audience effectively? The key is to fish where the fish are. Identify the platforms where your audience spends their time and engages with content. This could be social media channels like YouTube, Facebook and Instagram, or other avenues like email campaigns, sales funnels, or even in-store displays. The choice of platform should align with where your audience is most likely to engage with your content at the right stage of their customer journey.

Step 5: Choose what to optimise for success (1 minute)

Publishing your video is just the beginning. To ensure its success, you need to consider optimisation tactics that will help your video perform well on your chosen platforms. This could involve optimising thumbnails, titles and descriptions, leveraging existing networks to drive traffic, or integrating your videos into broader marketing campaigns. Effective implementation of these steps ensures that your videos not only reach but also engage your target audience.

Step 6: Define your metrics for success (1 minute)

This step is essential for evaluating the effectiveness of your video strategy. Look back at your goals and determine the KPIs that will help you measure success. This could include hard data like video views, click-through rates and sales conversions, or soft data like brand perception and audience sentiment. By setting clear metrics, you can track progress and make informed decisions to optimise your strategy further.

Step 7: Plan your video production (1 minute)

The final decision in the 7-minute Video Marketing Strategy is about the actual production of the videos. Based on the previous decisions, determine the format, style and budget for your videos. Whether you opt for professionally produced content or a DIY approach, the key is to ensure that your videos align with your strategic goals and resonate with your audience. The decision about production should always come last because it is a direct result of the strategic planning done in the previous steps.

While, in reality, the 7-minute Video Marketing Strategy might take you a little longer than seven minutes, it should become a guiding tool that simplifies the complex process of video strategy planning into seven key decisions. By following this structured approach, you can ensure that your video marketing efforts are aligned with your business goals, target the right audience and are set up for success. As you implement this plan, remember that each decision builds upon the previous one, creating a cohesive and effective strategy that drives meaningful results for your business. With this plan, you can confidently create and implement a video strategy that maximises your ROI and helps your business thrive.

BONUS MATERIAL

For downloadable worksheets and resources, head to *engagevideomarketing.com/more*

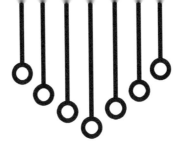

CHAPTER 16

The One Page Video Strategy Canvas

The 7 Minute Video Marketing Strategy process can be a great, simple first step however the next tool I want to share with you to add confidence to your role as a Video Strategist is a powerful single-page template that can be easily adopted into any business. This one-pager has become a go-to resource for many of my Video Strategy students over the years, and is a template we still use today in my video strategy agency.

I call it the One Page Video Strategy Canvas.

It's a strategic planning template allowing you to map out and document a clear direction for each video you produce. It also serves as an actionable reference tool that outlines video-specific decisions across the seven key elements that you are now familiar with as you've moved through this book:

1. Audience
2. Goals
3. Content

4. Distribution

5. Optimisation

6. Metrics

7. Production.

I designed this framework based on the famous Business Model Canvas methodology which was originally created as a visual chart of nine business building elements by Alex Osterwalder in 2005.

Just like the Business Model Canvas enables entrepreneurs to design and communicate business models on one page, the One Page Video Strategy Canvas empowers you to strategise and share video strategy plans with simplicity and clarity.

By guiding you to make decisions within those seven elements, this one-pager ensures you develop videos with purpose and intention. It compels you to consider target audience, intended reactions and actions, distribution channels, optimisation opportunities, success metrics and production plans. Instead of treating video as an isolated creative endeavor, this canvas facilitates an integrated, strategic approach—so your video content effectively contributes to overarching marketing and business development goals.

Let's take a look at the full One Page Video Strategy Canvas included on the next page.

ONE PAGE VIDEO STRATEGY CANVAS

VIDEO TITLE

DESCRIPTION

BUSINESS

PUBLICATION DATE

AUDIENCE

Primary Avatar

Key Demographics

GOAL

Intended audience action from video

☐ Brand Positioning (TOFU)

☐ Social Engagement (MOFU)

☐ Conversion (BOFU)

☐ Delight (ADV)

DISTRIBUTION

Initial release ☐ am / ☐ pm on ☐ M ☐ T ☐ W ☐ T ☐ F ☐ S ☐ S

Primary Channel	Secondary Channel	Lead-in Channel(s)
☐ YouTube	☐ YouTube	☐ Facebook
☐ Facebook	☐ Facebook	☐ Instagram
☐ Instagram	☐ Instagram	☐ IG / FB Stories
☐ LinkedIn	☐ LinkedIn	☐ YouTube Shorts
☐ Twitter / X	☐ Twitter / X	☐ LinkedIn
☐ TikTok	☐ Embedded	☐ Twitter / X
	☐ TikTok	☐ Snapchat

Supporting Content Plan ie. Blogs, eDM, Networks, etc

Other Notes:

PRODUCTION

☐ Production Company ☐ % Outsourced ☐ DIY / Internal

On Camera Talent

Camera / Production Logistics

Engagement Motivator

(What will motivate your intended avatar to engage with this content?)

CONTENT

Video Type

Topic / Theme

Purpose (4–5 keywords)

OPTIMISATION

Hook Strategy

Keywords

Optimised Title

Thumbnail Text / Concepts

Playlist or Hashtags

Description / Post Copy

Placement

Shoot Location

Desired Action Trigger

(What will trigger your intended avatar to take the desired action after watching this video?)

Aspect Ratio

Burnt in captions ☐ Yes ☐ No

Duration

Timeliness ☐ Current
☐ Evergreen

METRICS

Select relevant primary and secondary metrics.
Add your own where needed.

Reach	Engagement	Conversion
☐ Views	☐ Retention	☐ Leads
☐ Impressions	☐ Likes	☐ Sales
☐ Page Traffic	☐ Comments	☐ Traffic
☐ Email Open %	☐ Shares	☐ CTR
	☐ Sound On views	☐ CPA

Retention	Audience	Other
☐ Lifetime Value	☐ Demographics	☐
☐ Referrals	☐ Playback location	☐
☐ Repeat	☐ Playback device	☐
☐ Purchase rate		
☐ NPS		

Budget

ENGAGE

Completing the One Page Video Strategy Canvas

Before demonstrating how to put this canvas into practice, let's briefly cover how the seven elements are mapped out on this page, and get clear on how each section works with the next.

- **Audience:** Who specifically are you creating this video for? Detail target audience demographics and psychographics here—including any customer avatars developed. What will motivate them to actually watch and engage? Note any emotional triggers or framing mechanisms.

- **Goals:** What marketing goal does this video aim to achieve? Consider brand awareness, social engagement, conversion and delight. What exact action do you want viewers to take after watching? Feel, think or do something specific?

- **Content:** What information or message will you share to spur the desired action? Outline topic, purpose and format.

- **Distribution:** On what online platforms and channels will you publish this video? Detail paid and organic distribution plans.

- **Optimisation:** What specific optimisations will you leverage to maximise viewership and impact once video is live?

- **Metrics:** How will you accurately measure the success and ROI of this video? Select quantitative and qualitative KPIs.

- **Production:** What will the video production process look like? Production style, roles, equipment, budget etc.

Now let's take a look at a completed template outlining how one of our clients used this document to design a clear strategy for one of their ongoing video projects.

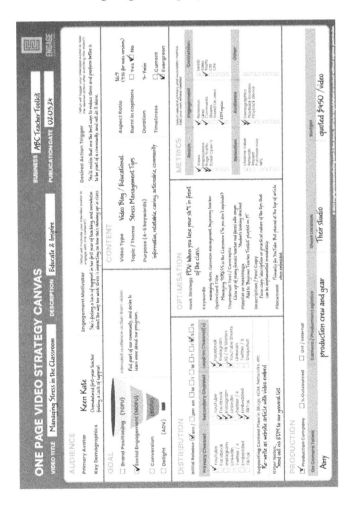

This client is a consultant who provides coaching, education and training to teachers just starting out in their careers. A core part of her digital marketing strategy involves publishing valuable video blogs on YouTube and Facebook, covering topics relevant to new teacher challenges.

These videos aim to:

1. Establish her expertise and credibility in the beginner teacher niche

2. Nurture organic community engagement and brand affinity

3. Promote her paid consulting and training programs.

For one of these videos focused specifically on 'Managing Stress in the Classroom', we mapped out the strategic decisions and plan on the One Page Video Strategy Canvas.

- **Audience:** We know our core target persona for most content is 'Kate', a 23-year-old first-time female teacher feeling overwhelmed. By tapping into Kate's pain point around classroom stress and her need to feel supported in-career, this video will strongly resonate. The desired trigger is for her to feel she's not struggling alone.

- **Goals:** This targets the social engagement goal of nurturing community. We want viewers to subscribe and share with other new teacher connections.

- **Content:** As part of our vlog series, this is a 5-7-minute educational video. It will provide stress management tips so teachers feel empowered and supported.

- **Distribution:** YouTube is the hero channel for launch. We'll also share natively on Facebook, repurpose short versions across Instagram, Instagram Stories, LinkedIn and Snapchat. An email nurture sequence and blog post will embed the video too.

- **Optimisation:** On YouTube, we'll leverage keywords teachers search like 'managing stress', 'classroom management' and 'first year teaching stress'. The title will be 'Tips for Managing Stress in the Classroom (So You Don't Explode)'. Thumbnails will display text like 'Managing the stress of teaching'.

- **Metrics:** Primary success metrics are YouTube views, retention, shares and subscribers. For Facebook, we'll track views, retention, likes, shares and comments. We'll also monitor engagement within wider new teacher online communities.

- **Production:** As this is for our own channel, we'll produce the video in-house. The client will feature on-camera in our green screen studio. We allocated budget from our fixed monthly content production retainer.

This One Page Video Strategy Canvas example showcases just how effective this tool is for mapping out clear strategic direction for a single video, while keeping aligned to the overall channel and business goals.

Putting your canvas into practice

Now you understand what the One Page Video Strategy Canvas framework looks like in a real-world example, let's cover some tips for effectively putting this tool into practice.

- **Use in pre-production client strategy sessions:** If you're consulting as a Video Strategist or an in-house marketer responsible for your video strategy, then I suggest you print these templates to bring to initial kick-off meetings with clients or your team and fill out relevant sections together. This gets you strategising before creative stages, fostering alignment.

- **Share completed canvases internally:** After strategy planning sessions, share final canvases with internal or external production teams working on the video. This communicates direction without them attending strategy meetings.

- **Revisit before filming:** Right before shooting, review the canvas again to realign on strategy and planned optimisation elements, ensuring teams incorporate these intentionally during production.

- **Update based on performance:** This canvas documents your strategy before production, but you can update sections based on actual video performance after distribution. Let data then guide your future iterations.

- **Build a video strategy library:** File completed canvases for reference. Having a library showcases strategic thinking behind all past video content.

The One Page Video Strategy Canvas is your secret weapon for developing video marketing game plans that get results. Following this straightforward seven-element framework steers your creative decisions, spurs intentionality and ultimately drives results.

BONUS MATERIAL

For downloadable worksheets and resources, head to *engagevideomarketing.com/more*

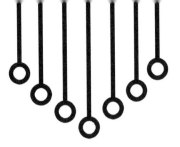

CHAPTER 17

The Simple 7

As we've clearly established throughout this book, video has become an indispensable tool for brands and businesses seeking to reach and engage their ideal audiences. Yet many shy away from embracing video fully in their marketing due to perceived barriers of production costs, time investment and the intimidation factor of appearing on camera. The truth is that readily accessible, affordable tools now enable any business to strategically incorporate video across the customer journey in authentic and effective ways. You don't need fancy equipment, large creative budgets or teams—just some DIY grit and the framework provided here.

Introducing the Simple 7

The Simple 7 is a purpose-driven video strategy model integrating seven easily produced video types mapped to essential stages of the Full Funnel Video Strategy Framework™.

This chapter details the model along with how embracing a 'low-tech, high-touch' video approach can drive results for your brand.

Video 1: Why Videos—Making an emotional connection

Leading with your purpose and values is how iconic brands inspire loyalty beyond products alone. As legendary marketer Simon Sinek suggests, people don't buy what you do but why you do it. Early in their journey, prospects seek that inherent alignment of beliefs before considering your offerings.

Why Videos answer what drives your business and how you help people. Keep it simple: use your phone selfie-style and speak genuinely about your motivations in less than 60 seconds. Don't sell, inform and inspire! Share via social channels, website headers or email signatures to forge trust and encourage emotional connection with your ideal customers.

Video 2: Success Stories—Crafting compelling narratives

When facts are woven into stories, people engage more and recall details better. Success stories relate client outcomes through an archetypal 'hero's journey': first immersed in a problem, then overcoming it via your guidance to ultimately transform their world. Structure customer success videos around five questions evoking key story stages:

- Who are you and what do you do?
- What key problem brought you here?
- Why did you choose us to solve it?
- How was the process of working with us?
- What results did you achieve?

Edit clips into polished testimonials or publish organic conversations directly. These simple but effective videos are incredible at inspiring engagement and building trust.

Video 3: Reels—Getting eyes on your brand

Harnessing the power of short-form video platforms represents a huge branding opportunity hiding in plain sight. As organic social media feed reach declines, unaffiliated yet engaging Reels occupy over 60% of the content Facebook and Instagram shows users today. Facing the camera or using creative visuals, businesses attracting mass attention once needed large followings or ad budgets. But not anymore!

Repackage helpful advice, behind-the-scenes glimpses, employee highlights or user-generated content into vertical micro-content. Natively publishing Reels feeds algorithm visibility, extending your reach exponentially through little ongoing effort. Be authentic and mobile-minded in messaging and stylistic approach. Think TikTok, not TV ads!

Video 4: AI Video—Automating an on-camera presence

Reluctance to be on video limits many from participating in this high-impact medium. Rapidly advancing AI tools like HeyGen, Syllaby and VEED now provide workaround solutions, from virtual talking avatars to automatically generated video scripts and graphics. Most offer free trials too!

At the rate that AI tools are developing, when you're reading this book chances are there are countless other options available to you right now as well.

While AI won't completely replicate the authentic connection viewers want from real humans, it does enable valuable, scalable content without physically appearing on camera yourself. Explore these emerging tools, but lead first with purpose over novelty. I suggest using these videos as a supplemental content form to get yourself or your team on camera authentically.

Video 5: Sales FAQs—Accelerating buying decisions

With 57% of purchase consideration formed prior to directly contacting your business, prominently answering frequent questions on-demand can make or break sale readiness. Self-directed online research drives 67% of the average decision journey. Videos addressing potential customer concerns condensed into snackable formats provide information precisely when needed, building crucial familiarity and trust.

Inventory your ten most repetitive enquiries, then create micro FAQ videos or batch commonly covered topics into a core sales video. Publish on conversion-centric landing pages, embed in your sales sequences or link through proposals. Machine-like efficiency meeting human needs—that's the goal!

Video 6: Quote Walkthroughs — Explaining and reassuring

You deliver exceptional proposals, but prospects often have lingering doubts or confusion. Rather than leave them anxious, use personalised screen-recorded walkthrough videos detailing your unique solution for their situation. Demonstrate line-by-line how you'll address root issues while also guiding decision makers who haven't been along for the full journey.

Tools like Vidyard, Loom and BombBomb simplify capturing this style of screenshare video. Key sections to cover include the project approach, specific deliverables, investment breakdown, expected results, terms and next steps. Proposal explanation videos can increase buyer willingness to pull the trigger by over 25%!

Video 7: Personalised Videos— Delivering high-tech, high-touch service

As we've moved from a high-touch, low-tech world of business into these days a very much low-touch, high-tech way of doing things, there is one key casualty for all this technology: meaningful human relationships. As personalised attention didn't scale profitably before, it faded from priority. Now advanced tools granting individualised connection finally offer the best of both worlds, if applied.

Short personalised video messages surprise and impress at each customer milestone: prospecting, sales meetings, post-purchase check-ins, implementation guidance, troubleshooting, restock reminders, real-time support, reorders, advocacy requests, etc.

Introducing personalised video into your sales and customer support processes can be a game-changer in bringing the human touch back into your customer's experience with your business.

Imagine sending a personalised thank you video to a customer after a purchase, addressing them by name and expressing genuine gratitude for their business. This not only makes the customer feel valued but also builds a stronger emotional connection to your brand. Similarly, sending a personalised video update during a project's progress can reassure clients that their needs are being actively managed, increasing their confidence in your services.

The Simple 7 should be technically simple too

Starting with video marketing through The Simple 7 framework doesn't require a major investment in professional equipment either. Most modern smartphones are equipped with high-quality cameras that can produce excellent video content. To enhance your videos, consider investing in a tripod for stability, a microphone for clear audio and basic lighting equipment to ensure your face is well-lit and visible.

Scripting and storyboarding

Before you hit record, take some time to plan your video. Create a simple script or outline that covers the key points you want to address. For more complex videos, storyboarding can help you visualise the scenes and ensure that your video flows logically from start to finish.

Practice makes perfect

If you're uncomfortable in front of the camera, practice is key. Record yourself multiple times and review the footage to identify areas for improvement. Pay attention to your body language, eye contact and tone of voice. The more you practise, the more confident and natural you'll appear on camera.

Editing

Although many of The Simple 7 video types don't require any editing at all, there are numerous user-friendly video editing tools available that can help you polish your videos. Programs like iMovie, Adobe Premiere Rush, CapCut and Descript offer powerful editing capabilities without requiring a steep learning curve. Focus on creating clean cuts, adding text overlays where necessary and incorporating music or sound effects to enhance your video, but only where necessary.

The Simple 7 framework offers a versatile and accessible approach to video marketing that any business can adopt. By starting with authentic, purpose-driven videos and gradually expanding your video content to cover different stages of the customer journey, you can build stronger connections, foster trust and drive meaningful engagement.

The power of video lies in its ability to convey emotion, tell stories and create a personal connection with your audience. With the simple tools and strategies outlined in this chapter, I believe that anyone can overcome common barriers to video marketing and harness the full potential of strategic video for their business. So pick up your smartphone, get comfortable on camera, and start your journey with The Simple 7.

The results will follow, transforming both your external perceptions and internal confidence as you master the art of video marketing.

BONUS MATERIAL

For downloadable worksheets and resources, head to *engagevideomarketing.com/more*

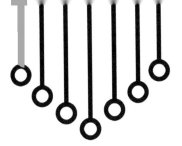

CHAPTER 18

Welcome Home Rentals Case Study

Kylie Best founded Welcome Home Rentals as a small business, operating initially as a one-woman show. From the outset, she recognised that one of the primary challenges of starting a business was gaining market awareness and establishing trust—an especially critical factor in the property management industry. Kylie understood that building a reputable brand required not only exceptional service but also effective marketing strategies to connect with her audience.

Embracing video marketing early on, Kylie leveraged this powerful medium to showcase her expertise, build credibility and create a personal connection with potential clients. This strategic move proved to be instrumental in growing Welcome Home Rentals into a leading property management company in her town. Eventually, her success and the strong brand presence she cultivated through video marketing led to a successful acquisition, allowing her to exit the business on a high note.

I'll let Kylie share her personal account of how video marketing impacted her business, providing valuable insights and lessons for other entrepreneurs looking to elevate their own brands.

Welcome Home Rentals had humble beginnings—like many startups, I couldn't afford anything that wouldn't fit on a shoestring budget. My lounge was my office and I was clear what I wanted to do. I wanted to take property management, dissect what had been done for decades, figure out how to do it far better and package that up into what clients needed and wanted.

Video was something I wanted to engage with quite quickly. I had seen (and admired) some colleagues' videos, and after watching a few do it really well, I recognised it was the quickest and most effective way to introduce myself to potential clients, especially as I had no shop front. I could literally get inside their home without ever being introduced in person.

What started out as a branding story, quickly became addictive. I always knew that if you want to sell your services to another person, you need to be able to give them something valuable. So being able to provide education on tenancy-related matters not only actually helped others (whether they were my clients or not) but it also positioned my business as being the industry expert. Show me a billboard and I'll show you money down the drain. Show me a great video and I'll show you a list of a repeat and raving client fanbase.

I don't think I had any preconceptions about video marketing. With social media really starting to ramp up as my own business did, videos were becoming more and more familiar and I liked being able to hear business owners speak, it made me feel like I knew them before I used their services.

Using video as a strategy was totally new for me. I had to really put myself in the shoes of my potential clients, switch places with them really, and think, "If I was you, what would I want to know?"

I got really interested about which content worked better than others. It made me realise I could still learn so much about what an investor really wants. Being able to engage with clients on a regular basis and use this as feedback for our business structure was really helpful to keep growing as a business in our structure and processes.

Our video library is quite extensive and a complete mix.

I have two branding stories. The first was when I was the home-based new kid on the block. The second was when our business moved to a shop front, had grown to five staff members and by that stage was recognised as the place to go for property management.

The brand stories led to Tradie Talk where I brought our tradespeople in for an interview. That was a beautiful cross-branding between the people who we rely on to fix things—our plumber, gas fitter, handyman, electrician and bond cleaner—while being engaging for our clients as well. It showed our clients how these businesses are essentially a part of ours.

From there, we used video for tenant and owner induction. This alone saved me thousands in wages and ensured we delivered consistent messaging to clients and tenants alike.

Our largest project was a series of Property Investor Videos which were all short, but highly informative, on all different topics from bond disputes, to why long-term tenants can be dangerous. (The latter of which turned out to be our most watched YouTube.)

Because of the consistency of the release of our videos, if a potential (or current) client missed one, they were continually seeing us pop up over their socials. Oftentimes, viewing one video would drive people to our YouTube channel and they would view more. Nobody else was doing anything like it so our brand awareness grew exponentially and quite quickly.

Because we were giving people something, information they often didn't know before, we became hot topic for anybody looking for a property management agency. Everybody who was a client was dying to tell their friends who just bought a property, "You have to see Kylie, she looks after ours and is fantastic." Through that recognition, we were able to capitalise on our return on investment by becoming more selective—choosing clients who were aligned with our value systems and core beliefs and also those with respectable homes rather than those you might see on A Current Affair!

An unexpected and really humbling sign of the success and value of our video material was to discover that not only were our videos being viewed around the world, they were also being utilised by recognised property management training organisations. Our videos were played in seminars and business coaches often referred to our content as examples of how to reach audiences and create engagement.

When I closed the chapter for Welcome Home Rentals and merged with Ray White, I made a beautiful transitional video. I have taken my passion for all things video into Ray White, and we have, to date, recreated a handful of our favourites.

Video, without a doubt, is hands down the best money I ever spent on my business. I truly believe that we wouldn't have grown to the size we did without it, it allowed us to keep working out of hours in that clients continued to see us even outside of normal business hours. We also attracted the clients we wanted with our content and, without needing to decline the business, we repelled those who didn't align with our values.

Our brand story and property investor series made us money, our induction videos saved us money. Rather than sitting down face to face with a tenant and explaining the terms of a lease, our tenants were required to watch our induction video and we discovered a program where we could track whether it had been viewed. The keys couldn't be released until it was, so if our tenant arrived but hadn't viewed the video, they had to sit through it in the office before they could go.

Through this, we found we had a lot less problems and issues—another money/time saver. We made ourselves clear on what was going to happen, rights, obligations, how to report maintenance, what our rent arrears procedure was. Everything was completely understood which eliminated (or at the very least highly minimised) the "I didn't know that" disagreements.

Clients are typically hard-working people. They don't have time to pop into the office and meet in person to go through the paperwork and there's page after page of things they don't understand. Although their video was optional, it gave clients the opportunity to have everything that they were signing explained in a way that made sense.

Video marketing took the new kid on the block to the business everybody wanted to manage their property. Even tradies and staff members wanted to work for us.

We set high expectations of ourselves and we genuinely wanted to deliver more, and be more. And that all showed in every video.

I tell anybody and everybody that if they want to build a successful business, they absolutely must prioritise video marketing. In fact, my cousin recently kicked off his own business and I insisted he do a brand story.

Every week he calls me with an update and almost every time he mentions how powerful that video is.

What I would say to anybody on the fence, or thinking they can't afford video marketing is this: if you think it's expensive, try building a business without it. It's too expensive not to.

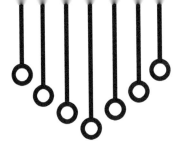

CHAPTER 19

Sticky Lollies Case Study

This story is one of how a business was saved through live video and short-form content.

The opportunity presented by social media and online video has allowed small businesses around the world to engage with customers in new and innovative ways. One of the most inspiring examples that showcases the power of live and short-form video content to grow and strengthen a small business is the story of Sticky Lollies, a boutique candy maker based in Sydney, Australia.

Sticky Lollies has been making handcrafted rock candy, gelato drops and other sweets in Sydney's iconic Rocks district for over 20 years. It started as a small shop attracting tourists and locals to walk in and watch the theatrical candy-making process. The business grew as they trained franchise operators in 11 countries and catered special events and weddings with customised candy. But COVID-19 threw an unexpected blow, nearly forcing them to close their doors for good.

Within a week in March 2020, as Australia enacted strict lockdowns, tourism vanished, events were cancelled, and Sticky Lollies' business went 'to zero pretty much instantaneously', said owner David King. As they scrambled for ideas to save the struggling shop, employee Lily suggested trying live video streaming on social media to showcase their production process.

With low entry barriers on platforms like Facebook and Instagram, going live and potentially reaching billions of users around the world was easy to try. They set up an iPhone against the shop window, fired up Instagram Live wearing silly costumes and started broadcasting their candy-making process—interacting with viewers in real time as mistakes happened and responding to comments.

'It just took off', said David. Engagement exploded as people globally found comfort watching their silly antics. Within a month 20,000 people were tuned into a single stream. A key driver of growth was allowing their innate theatrics and humour to shine in an authentic, unfiltered way that fostered community during a difficult time. 'People love it when you stuff up', David explained. 'They love it when you're human.'

Shortly after, David's daughter Annabelle suggested expanding to TikTok during its period of rapid adoption. She led creation of short-form behind-the-scenes and transition videos showcasing things like pouring and sculpting candy. These videos also went massively viral, earning millions of views, followers and shares across platforms.

Sticky Lollies didn't overproduce content or worry about perfection—the rawness and simplicity was key. 'I just don't overcomplicate it', said Annabelle. 'If I took a really good video of dad just making like a candy bubble and then popping it, I didn't need to go in and change how he looked or add screen overlays.' Letting mistakes happen and not being afraid to be themselves allowed authenticity and humanity to shine through.

The rapid growth in reach and followers forced changes, as online demand outstripped their manual order fulfillment system. Despite the logistical challenges, the social video strategy succeeded in saving the business during COVID—growing it three times in size since before the pandemic began. Beyond commercial success though, the greatest satisfaction has come from the supportive community coalescing around their business. Thousands in their Facebook group, many who were isolated and struggling themselves, share gratitude for Sticky Lollies helping them get through lockdowns with positivity. 'While I'm pleased the business has gone well, when I look back ... it's having that kind of community grow up around the business too that's been really satisfying', remarked David.

Some key lessons small business owners can take from Sticky Lollies' journey with social video include:

- Allow yourself to be human. Don't overproduce, edit out imperfections or strive for perfection. Let real moments shine through.

- Interact dynamically and foster community with live video. Making mistakes on camera endears you to viewers.

- Meet audiences where they already are on platforms—regularly experiment expanding video content types and styles.

- Share behind-the-scenes glimpses into your real work—give people the transparency and intimacy they crave.

- Stay true to your business strengths versus chasing short-term trends or altering identity. Community matters most.

Sticky Lollies was nearly another pandemic small business tragedy, but their embrace of live and short-form social video changed everything. Driven by relentless experimentation and always leading with their innate humanity, the results expanded far beyond business alone into a people-first community offering real connection, levity and sweetness despite constant uncertainty—ultimately transforming the trajectory of the business forever.

You can hear more about the Sticky Lollies story on episode 284 of the Engage Video Marketing Podcast. Go to engagevideomarketing.com/284

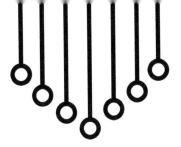

CHAPTER 20
NATPAT Case Study

Global ecommerce brand NATPAT's journey into the spotlight is a testament to the power of direct response video advertising. Founded by lifelong friends Gary and Michael, along with performance marketing expert Andrei, NATPAT quickly emerged as a prominent player in the market with their innovative product, BuzzPatch. This natural insect repellent in sticker form was conceived out of a personal need to find a fun, effective solution for their children who disliked traditional mosquito sprays. The founders' entrepreneurial spirit, combined with their shared experience and drive, led to the rapid development and launch of BuzzPatch during the early days of the COVID-19 pandemic.

The initial success of BuzzPatch can be attributed to a well-executed launch strategy that capitalised on their collective expertise. Within a few months, NATPAT's product was selling globally, supported by a robust direct response video advertising campaign. Central to their strategy was the emphasis on authenticity and the rapid testing of creative concepts. Real people using BuzzPatch were featured in their video content, which built trust and relatability. This approach aligned with a critical insight: authentic UGC often outperforms highly produced, professional ads. Consumers today value genuineness and are more likely to engage with content that feels real and uncontrived.

Andrei's role in performance marketing was crucial. By leveraging data-driven insights from Meta Ads Manager and Google, NATPAT continually refined their video content to discover what resonated best with their audience. This involved creating multiple variations of ads and closely monitoring performance metrics such as thumbstop ratio, click-through rates, landing page views, conversions and ultimately return on ad spend (ROAS). This iterative process ensured that their marketing efforts were always optimised for maximum results and continued sales growth.

A significant shift in Meta's advertising landscape influenced NATPAT's approach. Traditionally, the ad algorithm relied heavily on the setup of the ad campaign to find the ideal audience. However, recent changes have made the creative content of the ads the primary driver in audience targeting. NATPAT adapted swiftly to this shift, recognising the importance of compelling video ad creative in reaching and engaging their audience. Instead of relying solely on detailed targeting settings, they focused on producing high-quality, engaging videos that naturally attracted their ideal customers. This strategic pivot underscores the importance of strategic video creative in campaign success.

Innovation was another hallmark of NATPAT's strategy. They were unafraid to experiment with unconventional storytelling techniques and unexpected elements in their videos. This boldness kept their content fresh and engaging, capturing viewers' attention and maintaining their interest. Their willingness to test new ideas and rapidly adapt based on data-driven insights was a key factor in their success.

A significant part of NATPAT's success was their ability to adapt based on feedback from their audience. By actively monitoring comments on their ads and gathering feedback through email, they continuously refined their products and introduced new offerings. This feedback loop not only improved their product lineup but also informed their video content strategy, ensuring it remained relevant and effective.

'Listening to our customers has been one of the most important aspects of our strategy', says Andrei. 'Their feedback has guided our product development and helped us create videos that truly resonate with their needs and desires.'

Incorporating customer feedback into your video strategy can be a game-changer. Pay attention to the comments and messages you receive. Use this input to refine your scripts, address common questions or concerns and develop new video ideas that cater directly to your audience's interests.

The impact of NATPAT's direct response video advertising has been profound. They have doubled their sales on multiple occasions and secured partnerships with major retailers like Target in the US. Additionally, organic endorsements from high-profile influencers such as Kim Kardashian have boosted their credibility and expanded their reach. These achievements highlight the effectiveness of their video marketing strategy and its role in their rapid growth.

NATPAT's story offers valuable lessons for direct-to-consumer businesses looking to leverage video marketing. Authenticity in content creation builds trust and engagement, while continuous testing and data-driven decision-making optimise performance. The shift towards relying on ad creative for audience targeting emphasises the need for high-quality, compelling videos. By embracing these principles, NATPAT has demonstrated how direct response video advertising can drive rapid and sustainable business growth. Their journey is a powerful example of strategic video marketing in action, showing that innovation, adaptability and a focus on authenticity can lead to global success from a relatively humble beginning.

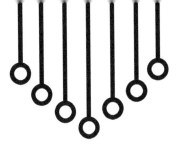

CONCLUSION
Your audience is waiting

It's now time to reflect on the journey we've taken and to consider how you can bring all the elements of an effective video strategy together to drive success for your business or clients. My goal in this final chapter is to synthesise everything we've learned and provide you with practical steps to implement these strategies in the real world.

First, let's recap the core concepts we've covered:

- **Audience:** Understanding your target audience's demographics, psychographics and behaviours is the foundation of any effective video strategy.
- **Goals:** Clear, actionable goals aligned with business objectives and the customer journey are crucial for guiding your strategy.
- **Content:** Developing engaging, valuable content across the full funnel that speaks directly to your audience's needs and desires.
- **Distribution:** Strategically choosing the right

platforms to publish your content ensures it reaches your intended audience.

- **Optimisation:** Controlling both audience and algorithm optimisation techniques to maximise the visibility and impact of your videos.

- **Metrics:** Tracking the right metrics to evaluate the success of your videos and make data-driven decisions.

- **Production:** Aligning production quality, budget and approach with the strategic needs of each video in your funnel.

When it comes to implementation:

1. **Start small, scale strategically:** Begin with a pilot project to test your strategy. Choose a single campaign or video series to implement all seven elements of the strategy. Monitor its performance, learn from the results and scale your efforts based on what works best.

2. **Leverage available tools and resources:** Use the templates, frameworks and tools provided in this book. These resources are designed to simplify the strategic planning process and help you stay organised and focused.

3. **Iterate and improve:** Video marketing is an ongoing process. Regularly review your metrics, gather feedback and be prepared to iterate on your strategy. Continuous improvement is key to staying relevant and effective.

4. **Stay informed:** The digital landscape is constantly evolving. Stay updated with the latest trends, tools

and best practices in video marketing. Join industry forums, attend webinars and follow thought leaders to keep your knowledge current.

In this book, we've explored various case studies and success stories. Reflect on these examples and consider how you can apply similar strategies to your business. Learning from others' experiences can provide valuable insights and inspiration for your own video marketing efforts.

My YouTube channel and podcast offer many inspiring stories:

- **YouTube:** engagevideomarketing.com/youtube
- **Podcast:** engagevideomarketing.com/podcast

As we look to the future, it's clear that video will continue to play a dominant role in digital marketing. Emerging technologies like augmented reality (AR), virtual reality (VR), and AI are already shaping the way we create and consume video content. Staying ahead of these trends and being open to innovation will ensure your video strategy remains cutting-edge and effective.

Embarking on a video strategy journey may seem daunting, but with the right mindset and tools, it can be incredibly rewarding. Remember, the most important thing is to start. Take the first step, implement what you've learnt, and be prepared to adapt and grow along the way.

As we close this book, I encourage you to put these strategies into practice. Start by creating your 7-minute Video Marketing Strategy and use it as a blueprint for your video marketing efforts. Share your successes and challenges with others, and continue to learn and evolve as a Video Strategist.

Now, go out there and create videos that engage, inspire and drive meaningful action.

Your audience is waiting.

BONUS MATERIAL

For downloadable worksheets and resources,
scan the QR code below.

engage

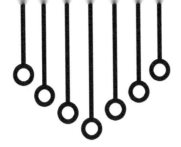

ACKNOWLEDGEMENTS

There are countless people who have had powerful influence on my professional life both as a business owner and a Video Strategist. There is simply no way to recognise everyone in this book, however ... I will do my best here to thank those that have helped bring the ideas and concepts in this book to life.

First, thank you to my book editor, designer and consultant Kelly Exeter for helping guide and shape these words and pages into the book you hold in your hands today. Thank you to my business mentors and coaches who have guided me over the years: Wade Grundon, James Schramko and Chris Ducker.

To my foundation VIPs (2016) and Bootcamp (2019) Video Strategists who trusted me to coach them when I was still finding my feet: Michael A, Michael J, Dave, Timothy, Marty, Anthony, Marcello, Rochelle, Glen, Rick, Jeff, Doug, Dennis, Jono, Jamie, Grant and Abi.

To every Video Strategist who has ever enrolled in one of my courses or programs from the Online Video Strategy Blueprint (The OGs), The Video Marketing Academy, The Strategy Board, The Video Strategists Masterclass or The Accredited Video Strategist Program.

To my friends and legends of marketing and business who contributed endorsements at the front of this book: Michael, Chris, James, Karen, Mel, Bill and Kate.

To my video business buddies and supporters over the years, particularly Ryan Koral and Den Lennie.

To my Innovate Media team: Doug, Matesse, Liam and also those who've moved on Zach, Adam, Braden and Taya. To Craig from Alaya Escape for the serendipitous location to finish writing this manuscript. To those who contributed their stories to the case studies throughout *Engage*, particularly Kylie Best, Gary, Michael and Andrei from NATPAT and David and Annabelle from Sticky Lollies.

To these people, and anyone I've missed, I say thank you. You're awesome.

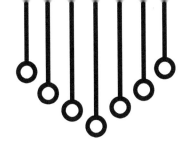

ABOUT THE AUTHOR

Ben Amos is a globally recognised Video Strategist, educator, speaker and content creator dedicated to helping businesses and video producers leverage the full potential of video marketing. As the Creative Director and Founder of Innovate Media, a video strategy and production agency  based on the Sunshine Coast in Queensland, Australia, Ben has collaborated with a diverse range of clients to develop strategic video content that resonates with audiences and achieves measurable results.

With nearly two decades of experience in the industry, Ben has become a trusted authority on video strategy. He hosts the Engage Video Marketing Podcast, a weekly show exploring the power of online video to engage audiences and move them to action. Through the podcast, Ben shares his expertise and interviews leading professionals in the field, providing listeners with valuable insights and practical advice.

In addition to his podcast, Ben offers expert training, coaching and consulting services to video producers, marketers and business owners. His mission is to equip individuals and organisations with the skills and confidence to elevate their video strategies, ensuring that their content not only captures attention but also drives meaningful engagement and business growth.

Ben's passion for video marketing is matched by his commitment to family. A devoted family man, he lives on the Sunshine Coast with his wife and two daughters. He regularly speaks at industry conferences and events, sharing his knowledge on topics such as personal branding in video marketing and the future of AI in video content creation. His insights have been featured in various publications, solidifying his reputation as a thought leader in the video marketing space.

Through his work, Ben continues to inspire and guide professionals in creating video content that not only looks great but also serves a strategic purpose, effectively engaging audiences and driving action.

www.ingramcontent.com/pod-product-compliance
Lightning Source LLC
Chambersburg PA
CBHW041639050326
40690CB00027B/5273